D0836861

PRAISE FOR PSYCHIATR

There is an epidemic of benzodiazepine overprescribing in America that is not being talked about. Long-term benzodiazepine use is associated with significant cognitive impairment, worsening anxiety, increased depression, sedation, increased risk of motor vehicle accidents and an increased risk of suicide.

Physical dependence can occur even among individuals who take their benzodiazepines exactly as prescribed and debilitating severe protracted withdrawal syndrome can last for months to years, and, in some individuals, may prove chronic.

Unfortunately, due to a lack of proper training in America, problems of physical dependence, tolerance withdrawal and severe protracted withdrawal syndromes are often unrecognized or misunderstood. Physicians may respond by increasing the patient's dose, misinterpreting the symptoms as evidence of another psychiatric diagnosis, tapering the benzodiazepines too quickly (often resulting in neurological harm), or abandoning these unfortunate patients altogether.

Physician awareness and education is desperately needed surrounding judicious prescribing and de-prescribing of benzodiazepines. This is an iatrogenic problem, created by Big Pharma and an epidemic of overprescribing, and it is our responsibility as prescribers to look at it honestly, with care and humility.

- Dr. Patricia Halligan, Board Certified Addiction Psychiatrist & Board Member of Benzodiazepine Information Coalition

In my forty years as a pharmacist, I've watched the over-prescription of benzodiazepines, which leads to patients requesting early refills at increasing dosages. Tapers can take months, even years, and can be accompanied with terrible, long-lasting withdrawal symptoms. I applaud Renée for her courage and her honesty in telling this important story.

- John Mazur, RPh & co-author of *Emilee: The Story of a Girl & Her Family Hijacked by Anorexia*

As a healthcare provider for over thirty years, I would never have believed this journey through benzodiazepine hell had it not also happened to me. I highly recommend all healthcare providers read this book. It will change the way medical professional practice medicine, which is a good thing because what we are currently doing is not working.

- Bobbi Wilkins, MPAS-PAC

What happened to Renée is, unfortunately, not uncommon. PSYCHIATRIZED will undoubtedly help many people suffering from benzodiazepine withdrawal. This memoir offers proof that it is possible for the brain to heal after an iatrogenic injury; it just takes a long time.

- Kristen Sullivan, NYS CARC

For decades, medical practitioners have been trying to treat emotional injuries with pharmaceuticals, and we are finally starting to see that this is just bad practice. In general, when healing emotional trauma, emphasis should be placed on healing naturally, with medication offered as a last resort. The imbalance in our mind, body and spirit is where illness begins – and it takes time for individuals to understand this to truly heal.

- Brette Key, LCC • Emotion Code Therapist & Life Coach

PSYCHIATRIZED

WAKING UP AFTER A DECADE OF BAD MEDICINE

RENÉE A. SCHULS-JACOBSON

STARRY NIGHT PUBLISHING
Rochester, New York

STARRY NIGHT PUBLISHING
Rochester, New York

Psychiatrized: Waking up After a Decade of Bad Medicine

A note to readers: This is a true story. Names and identifying details of some people portrayed in this book have been changed.

First Starry Night Publishing paperback edition August 2021

Cover design by Renée A. Schuls-Jacobson & Tony Zanni

Dedicated to the angels who helped me through,
that I might be an angel to those who are still suffering.

CONTENTS

AUTHOR'S NOTE

Over the last eight years, people have tried to convince me that the horrific experience I had weaning off clonazepam is unusual, that it was truly a most unfortunate "freak" accident.

As much as I wish this were the case, unfortunately, my story is *not* unique.

In fact, thousands of people all over the world have been injured while taking and/or coming off benzodiazepines like Xanax, Ativan, Klonopin and Valium.

Short-term, benzos work – and their effect in reducing anxiety is undeniable; but if taken longer than 2-4 weeks, even exacty as prescribed, a person can become physically dependent on the drugs without realizing it. Over time, benzodiazepines cause functional brain changes including cognitive impairment; perceptual and sensory disturbances; problems with digestion, balance, and hearing; as well as hypersensitivity to touch, smell and light. These impairments can last a long time, and – in some cases – it is suspected that the damage may be permanent.

Hundreds of articles, websites and blogs are devoted to supporting people who are currently trying to cope with the excruciating physical, emotional and psychological symptoms associated with protracted benzodiazepine withdrawal.

In the United States, iatrogenic injury is not new. At the turn of the 20th century, for example, drug makers paired highly addictive products with no government oversight or regulation, which was good for sales but dangerous for the safety of the general public. At that time, doctors and pharmacists assured customers that barbiturates were harmless based on information distributed by the drug makers, but the drug companies neglected to include information about how barbiturates "produced tolerance and dependence, and carried a high risk of overdose." [1]

History repeated itself in the mid-1950s, when researchers replaced barbiturates with a new class of drugs that were supposedly "cleaner," the benzodiazepines. Almost immediately, it was suspected that benzos – like the barbituates before them -- were also associated with debilitating side effects and withdrawal symptoms. And even though these suspicions were confirmed in the mid-1970s, general practitioners, psychiatrists and neurologists have continued to ignore warnings about the dangers associated with long-term benzodiazepine use and still broadly prescribe these drugs to individuals of all ages.

In 2019, an estimated ninety-four million benzodiazepine prescriptions were dispensed from U.S. outpatient pharmacies, with most patients having been prescribed benzodiazepines for years rather than the recommended 4-week maximum. [2]

If these numbers are accurate, we are already in the throes of a benzodiazepine epidemic, which foretells a future problem that has not been conceptualized – especially since the latest research indicates that psychiatric drug withdrawal can be "long-lasting and severe." [3]

For decades, the general public has been given the impression that psychiatric disorders are caused by "chemical imbalances" in the brain, and that psychiatric drugs fix those imbalances, just as insulin does for diabetes. Patients have been reassured that psychiatric drugs are safe, effective and often need to be taken for life. But what can be seen today is that this narrative was a marketing story, not a scientific one.[4] It was a story promoted by psychiatry and pharmaceutical companies for profit. In fact, psychotropic drugs do not fix "chemical imbalances"; instead, they disrupt normal neurotransmitter function.

In 2020, the United States Food and Drug Administration made a major admission about benzodiazepine drugs, acknowledging that patients can become "physically dependent" on them after taking them for as little as several days. They acknowedged that stopping the drugs abruptly or reducing the dosage too quickly can cause severe withdrawal reactions, "including seizures which can be life threatening," and stated that severe withdrawal side effects can last from "weeks to years." With more than 300,000 complaints about benzodiazepines logged into the FDA's Adverse Event Reporting System, this admission is long overdue.[5]

Over the last few years, it has become painfully obvious to me that psychiatry has taken a wrong turn when it comes to medicating human emotions with phamaceuticals. Prescribers need to be better educated about the role that trauma plays in their patients' lives, instead of being so quick to make a diagnosis and write out a script. Non-pharmacological treatments deserve more attention, and patient feedback must be taken seriously.

At one point or another, we all experience stressful life circumstances. We might lose a loved one, go through a painful divorce, or wrestle with an illness or injury; we might be forced to uproot ourselves and move far away to begin a new career. If we are fortunate, we have friends and family members to lean on to help us through these trying times; however, not everyone has these kinds of supports to fall back onto, and perhaps we find ourselves too embarrassed or too afraid to ask for the help we need. It is during these vulnerable periods that many of us end up "psychiatrized" and poly-drugged, sometimes for the rest of our lives.

It is my hope that this book will lend legitimacy to those who are suffering from protracted benzodiazepine withdrawal, a syndrome that causes severe long-term disability and is still not widely recognized by those in the healing professions. I want people who have been injured by prescription psychiatric drugs to understand that it is possible to heal after iatrogenic injury.

Finally, it is a goal of mine for people in protracted benzodiazepine withdrawal to receive better care than is currently the norm. None of us should have to fight so hard to receive the compassionate care we deserve.

PART ONE
CATERPILLAR

CHAPTER 1
CHEATED

My one and only pregnancy is difficult right out of the gate. The recommended prenatal vitamins do not seem to agree with me, and when I ask my doctor about the nausea that continues well into my second trimester, he waves away my concerns. "You're too tense," he says, condescendingly. "Go home and have a glass of wine -- or two."

As if the nausea isn't stressful enough, a partial placental abruption a month before my due date lands me on bed rest for what turns out to be the remainder of the pregnancy. During my time at home, I watch television shows like *A Baby's Story* on The Discovery Channel, and I read books like *What to Expect When You Are Expecting*. Even though I'm by myself all day long, I don't feel alone; after all, I have my baby to talk to.

While cooped up inside, with little to do but watch my ankles swell, I think about my wishes and goals for before, during and after labor and delivery. I anticipate a drug-free, natural delivery, and it never occurs to me that anything at all could go wrong or that my birth plan might need to change in the moment.

Because I'm on bed rest, I'm not allowed to attend any of my Lamaze classes, and my friends are surprised when I tell them that I don't know anything about breathing techniques, acupressure, or reflexology.

My husband assures me that the nurses will be able to talk me through the entire experience, but I begin to worry that I'm going into this childbirth thing unprepared.

As it turns out, I'm right to be concerned.

• • •

My contractions begin on a hot August morning. According to the doctor's calculations, I have two weeks left to go until my due date, so I putter around the house, cleaning and cooking, and rearranging furniture in an effort to ignore what I assume are simply false labor pains. But when I find myself holding my breath and grabbing onto the kitchen counter to steady myself every few minutes, my husband and I decide it's probably a good idea to have someone take a look at me.

Upon arriving at the hospital, I learn my regular obstetrician is on vacation and that another doctor from the same practice -- a woman I've never met– will step in to deliver my baby.

Dressed in blue scrubs with a bright floral bonnet, Dr. Rachel Radford is warm and personable. Gentle and patient, I feel fortunate to have her in lieu of my regular obstetrician, who has repeatedly minimized my questions and concerns. After watching me labor for nearly three hours without much progress, Dr. Radford becomes more serious. "Your blood pressure is too high, and the baby's heart rate is too slow," she says attaching a monitor to my belly.

The contractions keep coming and they seem to go on forever. Time passes, and as I grow more exhausted, my pushing becomes less productive.

Dr. Radford looks at what appears to be a tiny television screen. Though most of her face is hidden beneath a sterile hospital mask, I see her eyebrows knit together with concern. "The baby is still facing up," she says. "I'd like to try to turn him."

I know that "face up" is the less favorable position for delivery, and I instantly grant Dr. Radford permission to attempt to shift things around. Up until this moment, I've done everything naturally, without any drugs; but when Dr. Radford inserts what I assume must be her entire hand inside of my body, I realize I can't take any more pain.

"Can we get her an epidural?" Dr. Radford asks.

It's a perfectly reasonable request. Most women who give birth in a hospital setting are given epidurals to help with pain management; however, due to a suspected allergy to lidocaine, the anesthetic that is commonly used to numb the area and prepare for needle insertion, I'm not a candidate for the procedure.

Since my vacationing OB/GYN has not made a note of this issue in my chart, Dr. Radford is forced to make a difficult decision right on the spot. Pausing to look up at the clock on the wall, she rubs her forehead with her wrist. "We're going to have to cut," she says.

Suddenly, there is an uptick in the intensity level.

There are already a lot of people in my room.

Me.

My husband.

Two nurses.

The doctor.

Now, another nurse appears along with a man in a short white coat; he injects something into the IV line attached to my arm. Hell-bent on delivering my baby "the right way," I beg Dr.

Radford to let me push one more time. She says something about "vacuum extraction," but I can barely hear her over the sound of whatever machine has been turned on.

Seconds stretch into infinity. With the next contraction, I feel the hot stretching of my flesh. I hear myself screaming, and I hold my breath as his shoulders make room.

He's here, I think as I watch Dr. Radford hand my son to a nurse.

During the course of the pregnancy, I've read enough books to know how important it is for mothers to hold their babies immediately after birth so they bond properly. "Can I hold him?" I ask the nurse who is off to the side, her back facing me.

But he is blue and floppy.

And he isn't crying.

The loud machine used to assist in my son's delivery is turned off, and I feel a rising sense of panic as I wait for someone to tell me what is happening. My husband, a doctor himself, is doing his best to stay calm, but I can tell from the look on his face that something is wrong. After a few minutes, I feel another contraction – the placenta being delivered, and I feel as though the apocalypse is taking place from within my body.

A nurse hustles my son away as Dr. Radford busies herself between my legs. She's picking up cloths and asking for extra sponges. My husband stands beside her, and I feel simultaneously embarrassed and disoriented.

Suddenly, the edges of the room melt around me.

The next thing I know, I'm hovering above my body, looking down at myself -- and the entire room -- from about ten feet above. I've got an aerial view of the white tile floor, I can see the top of Dr. Radford's flowered paper bonnet, and I'm staring straight down into one of those square pink, plastic hospital-order basins.

That's a lot of blood, I think to myself. *I wonder whose blood that is.*

This thought lasts only a moment as I feel myself being pulled away from the scene below and directed toward a dark tunnel, almost as if I'm on some kind of an invisible conveyor belt.

Initially, I'm not scared; in fact, I'm strangely relaxed as I float past three or four odd tiles way up high on the wall that don't quite match the surrounding tile work.

But then a shadowy figure materializes from out of nowhere and begins to swirl around me in a menacing way. *This can't be right*, I think as my body moves down the smoke-filled tunnel. I can feel I've entered a terrible void where angry spirits reside in some alternate state of existence. All at once, I'm boiling hot and freezing cold. An icy, heat chars the bottoms of my feet, and I'm certain I'm being reduced to bone, to ash, to nothingness.

I must've done something terrible to have landed here, I think.

Halfway through the tunnel, my body disappears from the waist down, and I put my hands out to my sides, grabbing onto the air, in an effort to stop myself from going any further. Dozens of furious phantoms whirl around me, and I realize I'm going to die – that I will never know motherhood, and I experience a sense of despair I've never known before.

While hanging suspended, I feel someone, or something, take me by the hand and pull me off the conveyor belt. It's a sensation I remember from childhood, that of having a protective adult step in to guide me away from a potential danger.

No, The Voice says.

• • •

And suddenly, I'm back.

Lying on a narrow bed in a room lit by a dull blue light, I have no idea where I am or how much time has elapsed. Unable to move my arms, my wrists are strapped to stiff white boards. "Am I dead?" I say aloud to no one in particular. My voice is husky, and my throat is sore.

A nurse pops her head around the corner. She is young and perky, and I remember the whiteness of her teeth in the darkness. "Well, hello there!" she says in a southern drawl, a particularly out-of-place accent in Western New York State. The nurse smiles and tells me I'm in the Intensive Care Unit and that, in fact, I am not dead at all. Then, she exits the room in a swish of white, leaving me to wonder where my husband is and if our child is dead or alive.

After what feels like a long time, the door to my hospital room swings open and my husband materializes, looking more exhausted than usual. I want Derek to kiss me, to touch me, to tell me everything is going to be okay, but he hesitates in the doorway as if someone has glued his shoes to the floor.

The nurse approaches Derek, takes his arm, and escorts him to my bedside.

It's a moment for us to connect.

Except we don't.

He doesn't kiss me. He doesn't hold me. He doesn't try to console or comfort me.

"I've been running back and forth between the Newborn Intensive Care Unit (NICU) on the 3rd floor to this ICU all night long," Derek reports. He tells me our son has stopped breathing several times, but that he is stable now. I listen to him complain about how tired he is, how hard the night has been for him. He doesn't ask me how I'm doing or how I'm feeling. Instead, he walks toward a stiff looking recliner at the foot of my bed and collapses into it.

I've always been a person who processes difficult times by talking them out with a trusted person. I want to tell my husband about my weird postpartum experience that occurred right before I was rushed to the operating room, but he is visibly annoyed and relates to me as if I am a problem patient. I do everything I know how to do to try to connect with him. Scooting over to the far left side in my tiny hospital bed, I pat the mattress and ask my husband to snuggle up with me.

"I'm more comfortable over here," he says. It is not the first time he has refused me the comfort of physical closeness and, though it hurts, his rejection is not new. A nurse comes to check my vitals, and by the time she leaves, Derek is sound asleep in his chair.

We'll have time together later, I think, as I pull the hospital-grade sheet up over my chin.

• • •

I wake the next morning to sunlight streaming into my hospital room. Derek has disappeared, and I assume he has gone to the NICU to check on our son.

A short time later, a nurse brings me a Polaroid picture of Cal. Sound asleep and wearing an oversized diaper, my baby's tiny belly is crisscrossed with wires that I imagine are attached to all kinds of machines and monitors. The nurse assures me that my newborn is healthy and, soon after, he is wheeled into my room in a Lucite bassinette. I cry happy tears of relief when I'm finally allowed to hold him for the first time.

A little while later, a lactation consultant pays me a visit, and she is elated when she sees my son latch onto my breast so easily. "Sometimes when women lose a lot of blood, they aren't able to nurse," she tells me. I know from the books I've read that nursing is the healthiest option for babies, that breast milk contains the perfect nutrition as well as immune-boosting benefits, and I know there are benefits for new mothers, too. I'm grateful to be able to nurse, but the experience is exhausting for both of us.

When Cal falls asleep in my arms, a nurse takes him from me and places him gently into the bassinette beside my bed. "You should get some rest too," she whispers, but just as I'm about to fall asleep myself, an attendant arrives with a tray of food for me to eat. After two bites of toast and a spoonful of yogurt, my breakfast is interrupted when yet another nurse comes into my room. Aggressively pushing my tray of food off to the side, she rolls a pair of tall, flesh-colored compression stockings over my feet and stretches them up until they reach just over my knees. "Time for you to get up and walk around a bit," she says.

As I shuffle down the hall with one hand against the wall, the nurse holds onto my arm with a vice-like grip. "You don't have to hold me," I say. "I'm okay."

But the nurse refuses to release my arm and watches me with the intensity of a baseball player awaiting a fly ball. "You lost a lot of blood," she says. "Sometimes when people lose a lot of blood, they pass out."

Though I don't experience the dizziness everyone seems to be so worried about, I'm worn out from my short walk around the Intensive Care Unit. Returning to my room, I climb into my bed and a nurse materializes to wheel Cal back to the NICU.

Though I've requested not to have any visitors, a nurse comes into my room to let me know that my mother and my brother's wife are outside. They have driven ninety-minutes to check on me, and after I agree to let them come in, I watch their wide, expectant smiles fade into something akin to fear. There are no mirrors in my hospital room, but I have seen enough of my reflection in the dull metal paper towel dispenser in bathroom to know that I am puffy from all the intravenous fluids administered just a few hours earlier. When my mother leans over to hug me, I try to smile, but I'm exhausted and can barely hold my head up.

From out of nowhere, Derek appears to escort my family out of the room. "I'll take you to see the baby," I hear him say as the door closes behind them.

It's strange being alone in my hospital room. For nine months, I've established a routine with my son on the inside of my body, and now with him outside, in the real world, I feel superfluous, like an empty vessel.

• • •

Two days after our son is born, Derek returns to work full-time. Because my red blood cell count is still very low, I'm not allowed to leave the hospital, and Derek makes arrangements with his mother to stay with me while he is away taking care of his own patients. My mother-in-law brings chopped liver sandwiches to me in the hospital -- "to replenish my iron levels," she says – and she sits with me for a few hours each day, which I appreciate.

It's been a long time since I've failed at anything, and my terrible experience in the delivery room somehow makes me feel like a failure as a woman. When I try to share these feelings with my mother-in-law, she showers me with optimism and platitudes. I know she means well when she tells me that everything will be fine, but I don't feel as though I'm being heard or understood. "By the time I was your age, I had three children of my own," she says. "Having babies was easy for me." While I know she doesn't mean to minimize my feelings, it is conversations like this one that leave me feeling ashamed for being "high-maintenance" and for requiring a costly, extended hospital stay.

In the evenings, there is a changing of the guard. My mother-in-law goes home, and my husband goes first to the NICU to check on our son and then he comes to my room to check on me. Exhausted after his full days at work, his visits are brief.

Several days pass and my blood count remains too low. Finally, after much discussion, it is determined I will not take a blood transfusion. Derek is concerned I could receive blood that has been contaminated with Hepatitis C or HIV, and he decides it would be best if I simply go home to heal naturally. Since I'm not in any condition to make well-informed decisions for myself, I turn over my medical care to my husband. He is a doctor, and I trust him to make good decisions on my behalf.

• • •

On the eighth day of my hospital stay, right before I'm about to be discharged, Dr. Radford comes into my room to attend Cal's circumcision. Because my husband and I are of the Jewish faith, rather than having someone in the hospital perform the procedure, a traditionally trained mohel comes to oversee our son's bris. Typically, the mohel would be the one to perform the circumcision, but because Derek is a medical doctor, our mohel offers him the opportunity to make the cut himself. It is a tiny gathering, and from my place on the bed, I watch my husband and his father hold down our son's tiny legs. A clamp is applied and, a moment later, the mohel hands over his scalpel to Derek.

I feel like Cal and I have been through enough, and while the circumcision is swift and uneventful, I'm glad when my son is back in my arms.

"There was a point where I thought I was going to lose you both," Dr. Radford says, wiping tears from her eyes. "I'm just so happy you're leaving the hospital as a family."

While I'm grateful to be alive and going home as a family, I'm stuck on the fact that nothing has gone to plan. On what should have been a day for balloons and flowers and singing and whooping it up, my newborn son and I both nearly die, and I feel cheated.

It was not part of my birth plan to have an atonic uterus, to lose nearly three-quarters of my blood, or to be rushed to the Emergency Room for a D&C. I find myself thinking about all the women of the world, how it is that most women give birth easily, sometimes in the most inhospitable settings – and I can't understand why our day had to be such a catastrophe.

I'm sore after the long delivery and subsequent surgical procedure, and I burst into tears when Dr. Radford informs me that I will have to resume bed rest once again, at least until my hematocrit is back within a more normal range.

Why is this happening? I wonder. I'd planned for people to marvel at my newborn infant at the grocery store. *"Up and around already?"* I'd imagined they'd say. I'd planned long, lazy, late summer walks with the fancy-schmancy new stroller, planned to take my son outside and show him the world, let him feel the August sun on his cheeks.

• • •

Before I leave the hospital, a personal care aide is assigned to help me in my home with the baby, the laundry, and the meal preparation. For three months, Sandra takes care of my son's most basic needs -- making sure he is fed and diapered and sleeping in his crib -- but she is hardly a warm personality. When I try to talk to her, she makes it clear she is there to work, not socialize. I worry that my son and I aren't spending enough time together, that we won't bond properly, and I feel lonely and forgotten holed up in the master bedroom by myself.

Meanwhile, everyone assumes I'm getting exactly what I need.

At the time, I think I am too.

But in reality, my deepest needs are not being met.

When I look back at it with the knowledge I now have, I understand that, in many ways, I didn't receive anything in the way of modern postpartum care. After the delivery was complete, my son and I were barely alive, but alive, which seemed to check all the boxes for a successful birth. I now know there are many dimensions of wellness besides the absence of physical pain: dimensions including emotional, social and spiritual needs that were not met on any level.

I entered the hospital with expectations. I thought my husband and I would spend long hours lounging around together, dreamily looking at each other and marveling at the incredible miracle that we'd created.

In reality though, we'd never had a single conversation about how our lives would need to change after we became parents, nor had we discussed what I might need postpartum. In truth, I had no idea that there was anything that I would need, and nothing could have prepared me for the feelings of disorientation and confusion that I experienced after my son's delivery.

• • •

Every new mother leaves the hospital postpartum with an invisible wound inside of her body that takes time to heal. Even women who have the easiest of deliveries experience massive physiological shifts as progesterone levels drop and suspensory ligaments that hold up the uterus recover. However, because all of these events occur internally, no one can see what is actually happening. We don't pay much attention to how our bodies feel and we generally ignore our organs unless there is a problem.

In my case, I lost more blood than is typical, and there is the physical trauma associated with a vacuum extraction. Worse than the physical pain, though, is the emotional pain I felt when I was abruptly separated from the child that had been living inside of me; when our nervous systems -- which had been inextricably, interdependently comingled -- were suddenly ripped apart.

The moment Cal was taken from my body, I began to feel an uncomfortable, jittery sensation that just won't seem to go away. There are both organic and inorganic reasons for this feeling. Some might point to the fact that I was anemic after losing so much blood and that lowered iron levels can cause the kinds of symptoms I was experiencing – and that is certainly true. Others might point to side effects associated with the anesthesia I was given – and science supports this explanation, too.

But there is more.

I am frightened by everything I've experienced in the hospital, and I have no one to process any of it with: no one to help me make sense of it all. In addition, in many ways, I feel like a failure. The high level of care that I require after the delivery reinforces earlier messaging that I am in some way defective as a woman. When I try to talk with my husband about how I'm feeling, it is obvious he doesn't want to hear about it. "Can't you forget about all that and just focus on your son?" he asks.

It is not the first time I have been asked to compartmentalize my feelings, and while I've been able to do it in the past, the truth is that my son's traumatic birth touches old wounds that I don't yet want to see.

I have a vague awareness that I need something else; something I'm not yet able to articulate. I'm craving a connection with my husband, a kind of deeper level intimacy that I assume he wants too.

But there is a void in our relationship, a chasm I do not want to see.

So I do what I've been taught to do.

I stay silent, put my husband's feelings before mine, and try to be accommodating.

CHAPTER 2
LIFE REVIEW

While at home recuperating after Cal's delivery, I find myself thinking about my life, about where I grew up and how I was parented, as well as how the events of my youth impacted the choices I later make as an adult.

• • •

Born and raised in an upper middle class Jewish family in Upstate New York, I have everything a girl could want. My father has a secure job that he loves, working as an Electrical Engineer at General Electric, and my mother -- once a full-time elementary school teacher – trades her career to become a full-time stay-at-home mother. Surrounded by extended family -- with grandparents, aunts, uncles and cousins all living nearby -- I have clothes on my back, food in my stomach, and a bedroom filled with toys and books. From the start, both of my parents are delighted by me, their first child. I am the apple of my father's eye. In fact, my earliest years are filled with much adoration from both parents, and I remember feeling genuinely loved and supported.

Throughout my elementary school years, I am independent, authentic and outspoken. I challenge rules and exercise strong critical thinking skills; I have plenty of friends and I am comfortable being in charge and at the center of attention.

As I move into middle school, my mother and I begin to have increasingly frequent squabbles. During this time she insists that I need to be agreeable, quiet and compliant. "Children should be seen and not heard," she often says. If I express an opinion that is not in complete alignment with hers, my mother belittles me and calls me names.

It's hard for me to think about the frequent spankings I endured at the hands of my most important caregiver. As much as I find myself wanting to sugarcoat it, the truth is that my mother regularly raged at me, hit me, and then either sent me to my room for hours or -- more frequently -- locked herself away in her own bedroom. I can vividly remember numerous times where I stood in the hallway, crying and begging my mother to open the door to talk to me. The feeling of being punished, of being ostracized and isolated from someone I loved and upon whom I was dependent created a kind of separation anxiety inside of me that negatively impacted my self-esteem and my sense of belonging.

As bad as the spankings were, they were made worse by the fact that when I reported to my father what was going on in his absence, he didn't believe me. "Your mother loves you," he always said, firmly taking her side. "She would never do the things you're saying." At the end of every conversation, my father tells me he loves me, and then urges me to try harder to be a 'good girl' and honor my mother, as commanded by the Torah.

As I grow older, I not only feel pressured to be "good," but I also feel increased pressure to be socially successful, academically excellent, smart, fit and pretty too. Whether I am at home, at school, or at synagogue, I am expected to put other people's needs before my own, to conform to the larger group, and to stifle my feelings. At gymnastics, if I fall off an apparatus or hurt myself, my coach tells me to "shake it off" and "just keep going."

Around this time, I start to struggle to understand abstract mathematical concepts and, for the first time, I feel less intelligent than others. When comparing myself to my peers, I always seem to come up short. I remember those years, feeling myself walking a treacherous line, balancing mixed messages about how far I should go and how strong I should be: I am to be enthusiastic, but not loud; smart but not opinionated; intelligent, but not a leader; brave, but not bossy. I am to be something, but not too much.

Things become more confusing when discussions about sexuality are thrown into the mix. Judaism is generally sex-positive, regarding sex as a divine gift and a holy obligation. At synagogue and at home, I am taught that sex is a natural, beautiful thing -- as long as it occurs between a man and a woman who are married. Abstinence is emphasized in my home, and it is made clear that a woman is "ruined" if she engages in sexual intercourse before marriage; however, the rest of the world shows me that relationships between men and women are far more complicated than is explained at home. Television shows me that everyone is "doing it" all the time, whether they are married or not.

In 1979, my gymnastics coach is found guilty of molesting nine girls aged 12 to 16. After his trial, he is sentenced to serve three concurrent three-and-a-half year terms in state prison. Soon after, the gym is closed permanently, and I am left confused about how someone I trusted could do something so wrong and seemingly out of character. Neither of my parents wants to talk about what has happened at the gym. My father seems to blame the coach, while my mother blames the girls and warns me about the dangers of being 'too fast.' "Those girls must've done something for that to have happened to them," she insists.

• • •

As a female growing up in the United States, the objectification and harassment of women is nothing new, and during the 1980s, this behavior is normalized in music videos, in movies, and in the dominant culture. The moment I enter high school, I'm subjected to much unwanted sexual attention by men who touch my body without permission, slap me on my bottom, make sexually explicit comments, and request sexual favors, to name just a few harassing behaviors. I don't like it, but everyone I know seems to be used to and accepting of being manhandled. "If a boy teases you, it means that he likes you," I am told, and when I try to advocate for myself or speak out against these practices, I'm teased and told to stop complaining about the way men behave, to accept their unwanted advances as normal, even as complimentary.

During high school, I feel sexually empowered. As a gymnast and dancer, I'm proud of my body and the way I move. Feeling strong, confident and coordinated, my first sexual experiences take place inside a serious relationship. Everything we do together is consensual, but I have this nagging sense of guilt about enjoying sex before marriage.

• • •

During the summer of 1985, just two weeks before I'm supposed to go away to college, I'm raped by someone four years my senior. The betrayal of trust wrecks me emotionally and, if the details of the night were not terrible enough, the fact that I am doubted by my closest friends and shamed by my family leaves me feeling abandoned, rejected, and generally unloved and sets the stage for how I learn to handle later trauma – which is to keep my feelings bottled up inside and not look for support from anyone else.

While I look "fine" on the outside, I most definitely am not. After years of abuse, of being shamed and silenced and made to keep other people's secrets, I truly believe that in addition to being unattractive and unintelligent, that I've been irreparably ruined sexually so no one will ever love me.

With these destructive messages firmly embedded in my psyche, I head off to college and, later, into the world. Up to this point, my only coping skill has been to actively ignore my feelings and keep moving. Being in school makes it me easy for me to stay busy; there is always another book to read or paper to write. To the outside world, it appears I'm doing everything right. I receive academic honors, win writing contests, and have poetry and prose published in various magazines. I graduate Phi Beta Kappa with a Bachelor's degree and, three years later, I earn my Master's degree, as well as a teaching certificate in Secondary English.

• • •

While attending graduate school, I meet a smart and funny medical student. We are both Jewish, and it doesn't take long for us to figure out that a lot of my friends from summer camp are people with whom he had attended high school.

One night, the two of us grab a bite to eat. Sitting outside my favorite Italian restaurant, I have no idea I'm on a date with the man who will become my husband. I think we are simply two friends having dinner, so while Derek can barely eat, I proceed to devour nearly everything off his plate.

"Are you not eating that?" I ask, pointing to his last few stalks of asparagus.

"You can have them," Derek says.

From the beginning, Derek feels familiar. I love him and I never doubt his love for me. He provides me with a calm life, filled with routine, and – for the most part – his routine fits mine. Our common areas – shared faith, devotion to family, appreciation for good friends, and interest in travel – make me feel connected to something bigger than just myself, and being with him makes me feel safe.

It doesn't bother me that Derek doesn't care for my favorite music; it doesn't matter that he doesn't like to dance or sing or go camping. I'm not worried that he holds a few opinions that are different from mine.

At the time, nothing seemed insurmountable. As far as I was concerned, there were no red flags or deal breakers.

Looking back at it now, though, I can see there was one area in which Derek and I were very different. I was (and still am) a sensual person who enjoys a lot of physical contact. Holding hands, sitting close, and snuggling up with a lover is about my most favorite thing in the world. While I was aware that I desired more closeness than Derek did, it didn't seem like that big of a deal. And while our relationship might not have been as passionate as some of my previous romantic relationships, ours felt like a grown-up kind of love, the kind that would grow deeper with every passing day.

Without any hesitation, I move with Derek to New Orleans, where he begins his first year of an ophthalmology residency, and I start my career as an English teacher.

Though our professional lives are busy, we always make time for shared adventures. Our dreams are completely aligned. After four years in New Orleans, Derek has many options regarding where he might go to practice medicine, but we decide together to return to New York State to begin our married life and be close to our families.

The birthplace of some of America's most iconic companies – including Kodak, Xerox, Bausch and Lomb, and Wegmans, to name just a few, Rochester boasts internationally known universities and plays an important role in both abolition and women's rights movements. With its highly educated workforce, Rochester is known for having a vibrant art and music community.

Often ranked one of the best places to raise a family due to its low cost of living, Derek and I are able to afford a nice home in one of Rochester's suburbs. I feel confident that by living in Derek's hometown, we will be able to depend on friends and family for help when the time comes for us to start a family of our own.

For a few years, everything runs smoothly.

In fact, up until my difficult labor and delivery, it seemed like nothing could ever go wrong.

CHAPTER 3
SLEEPLESS

After eight weeks of bed rest, my blood is tested and a determination is made that I'm fine. My personal care aide is dismissed, and I'm left to care for my newborn, alone, for the first time. Having been stuck inside for months, I'm eager to finally go outdoors. It's October now and the autumn leaves fall from the trees and crunch beneath the wheels of our new stroller.

When I start my stint as a stay-at-home mother, the expectation is that I am supposed to love it. Everyone tells me staying at home full-time is a luxury and that I am lucky to be able to afford to do it.

And there are parts I do love. I love putting my son down on a soft, flannel blanket and playing him my favorite music, watching him kick his legs, seemingly to the beat. I love watching him eat. Cal is precocious and develops outstanding fine-motor skills by seven months, and I marvel at the way he can track one green pea, corner it, pinch it between his thumb and forefinger, and bring it easily to his mouth— never once dropping it. I love the way he giggles when I blow raspberries on his belly. I love that he learns things quickly and is easily disciplined.

But from the moment I come home from the hospital, I develop an unhealthy relationship with sleep. Initially, I assume my insomnia is due solely to having a newborn in the house – and everyone reassures me that this is normal -- but over time, there seems to be a secondary cause. At night, I lie awake, listening to Derek's breathing, calm and even, and I'm filled with that same nervous energy that I had in the hospital, coupled with a feeling of dread.

Over time, with less sleep, I become more volatile. By day, I am a bundle of activity – cooking, cleaning and worrying over my son. People tell me to sleep when the baby sleeps, but somehow, I'm not able to do it. Every afternoon, I clean the house in anticipation of Derek's arrival after work. I know he likes the house tidy and dinner made. It's hard for me to balance having a baby and taking care of the household, and it seems I never have a moment off.

When Cal is about a year old, my husband and I have one quick discussion during which time it is decided that it would be best if I continue to stay at home full-time. "You've got your master's degree," he says. "You can always go back to teaching when he's a little older."

I'm not completely on board with this plan, and I ask my husband if he will consider coming home from work early one day a week so that I might be able to get out of the house to have a little time to myself, or so that we can have some time together. In truth, I still haven't fully recovered from Cal's traumatic delivery, and I can't imagine going back to teach full-time feeling the way I do at this moment.

"Don't be ridiculous," he says. "I can't do that."

I know better than to argue.

When I inform my department chair that I won't be returning after my maternity leave expires, she has harsh words for me. "You're making the biggest mistake of your life," she says. And while I don't miss the meetings or the calls to the parents, I miss feeling like I have a larger purpose than simply washing the laundry or the dishes, which only get dirty and need to be washed again.

Outwardly, I smile and appear to be well put-together, but privately, I feel something akin to a glass of water only half-full. Living at the top of a hill, in a beautiful house, in the suburbs, I feel disconnected from friends and family. I don't know my neighbors, and I feel rudderless without a community. For the first time, I realize Rochester is not my hometown and that I'm going to have to make new friends to help me navigate my new job as a full-time stay-at-home-mother.

During this time, I spend a lot of energy trying to make our 1970s fixer-upper feel like home, and I'm forever rearranging the furniture, organizing and re-organizing the spices in the pantry, changing around the knick-knacks, trying to make our outdated kitchen look more appealing, and slowly peeling dated foil paper off the walls.

While Cal takes his daily nap, I pour myself into project after project, but after the walls are washed clean and the rooms are painted, that uncomfortable, buzzy feeling stirs up, like flames out of embers.

Where once my husband and I had been equals, we now have a sharp division of labor. He is the breadwinner, out in the working world— and I am the keeper of home and hearth. *Motherhood has destroyed my brain,* I think to myself, remembering a wool sweater I'd once thrown in the dryer that came out one-third its original size.

"Of course you feel this way," everyone tells me. "The baby is little. It will get better."

Except it doesn't.

Months pass and my insomnia worsens. Long after my son begins sleeping through the night, I don't seem to be able to get back into the groove of things. Sleep, which has always come naturally for me, is now an elusive gift, always just out of reach.

Around this time, Derek begins to spend more time away from home. After eating dinner, he falls asleep in front of the television, while I put our son to sleep and climb into bed exhausted. Lying there alone, craving connection, my brain whirs to life. I make elaborate lists that I run through again and again. When I do manage to fall asleep, I'm haunted by strange memories and recurring nightmares.

During this time, everyone has advice to offer. "You could be suffering from anemia or some other vitamin deficiency," I'm told repeatedly. People assume the cause of my insomnia is physiological in nature: no one considers the fact that I could be suffering from post-traumatic stress as a result of my son's delivery, and no one validates my feelings of extreme emotional and social isolation.

Years pass. Friends and family assume I've completely healed and that I'm finally back to baseline. I want to believe them, but it's not true. My brain creates a plausible storyline that my symptoms are the result of boredom as opposed to emotional, intellectual, social or spiritual deficits, and I decide that everything would be better if I could just return to teaching.

When I tell my husband that the stay-at-home thing isn't working for me, he's perplexed. "I'd kill to be able to stay at home with our son," he says.

I try to explain it to him—how I feel alone in our house on the hill; how I love our son madly, but I need to connect with people and things outside our family—how I have too much anxious energy and I don't know what to do with it. "I feel like we aren't connecting either," I tell him.

At this point, the two of us haven't been intimate in over a year, but every time I bring up our love life, my husband changes the subject or walks into another room. The more I press the issue, the more he backs away. I internalize his avoidance as a personal rejection, and I'm reminded of the way I used to feel when I was young, when my angry mother would retreat to her bedroom and lock the door, effectively shutting me out.

Feeling sad and frustrated, I make an appointment to speak with the rabbi at our synagogue about what is happening in my marriage. I tell him about the pressures of Derek's job, how busy and tired he is. We talk about my feelings of loneliness, and I ask the rabbi if my desire to have sex is unreasonable, and he assures me it is not. "The Torah commands a man to pleasure his wife on a regular basis, if she desires it," he says.

"What if he won't?" I ask. "Or if he can't?"

The rabbi smiles. "You're a pretty girl," he says. "And if you're a good teacher, I'm sure you'll be able to pull him out of his shell."

I can feel my cheeks redden. According to the rabbi, if my husband is not interested in sex, then clearly I'm not doing something right. I vow to try harder, to be a better teacher.

"Do yourself a favor and find something else to occupy yourself," the rabbi says. He advises me to find activities that will fill me with joy and tire me out. "Everyday activities help repair the world," he says. "Try not to focus on what you are missing."

In response to the rabbi's suggestions, I join a gym and a women's group; I take on a freelance writing project and try to busy myself with creative outlets. But at the end of each day, I still find myself craving intimacy, connection and affection. When I try to cozy up to my husband, he turns to face the wall of windows. "I'm exhausted," he says. I know he has a full day of surgery the next morning; he has told me many times. Lying awake beside him in bed, I hold in my tears, as I know that even the slightest sound or movement will disturb him.

Somewhere over the course of my life, I've learned to make myself small and quiet in relationship and to prioritize my husband's comfort and happiness over my own.

• • •

When Cal turns two years old, I'm still sleeping less than four hours a night, and I begin to dread the sun going down. I stay up late working on writing projects, hoping that eventually my eyes will grow heavy and that I'll simply fall asleep. One night, it is well past midnight when I finally go upstairs. As I settle into my warm covers, I press my body up against my husband, hoping he will respond favorably to my advances.

Having been asleep for hours, Derek is not feeling at all amorous, and he uses both hands to push me away from him. It is the first time he has done something like this, and I feel as though I've been kicked in the stomach.

Suddenly, I hear a voice.

You've got to go, it says.

I lay there for a long while, waiting to hear if the voice would repeat itself, and when it does, I climb out of bed and walk over to the brick chimney in our master bedroom.

“What are you doing?” Derek asks.

“I hear whispering?” I say, pressing my ear against the bricks. “Do you hear it?”

Derek doesn’t hear anything. He tells me he’s worried about me and suggests that I make an appointment with my primary care physician, which I do the very next day.

Dr. Sparks has been my doctor for many years, and I trust him when he tells me that my insomnia is anxiety related. “You have a young child,” he says. “Of course you’re tired.” Dr. Sparks reassures me that my lack of sleep can be easily remedied with medication. When I express distaste at the idea of taking a psychiatric drug, he smiles at me gently. “Everyone is taking a little something these days,” he says as he writes me a prescription for Prozac, a commonly prescribed antidepressant.

Within twenty-four hours of starting the medication, I begin to experience muscle spasms in my legs as well as a facial tic. “Can you see my eye twitching?” I ask my friends. Sometimes they say they can, but most of the time my symptoms are invisible.

Dr. Sparks encourages me to try one antidepressant after another, in quick succession, each one revving me up more than the last. After three failed attempts with different selective serotonin reuptake inhibitors (SSRIs), I decide to stop looking for a pharmacological solution. The medications make me feel worse, and put me further from my goal of getting restorative sleep. For one year, I try to manage the insomnia on my own, but eventually I am forced to reach out to Dr. Sparks again.

CHAPTER 4
CHOKING

In January of 2004, I begin to feel a weird tightness in my throat, which feels like I have swallowed a pebble. The sensation becomes so intense that I feel like I am choking all of the time. As the nurse weighs me and checks my vitals, I think about how many years I've not been feeling right.

"One hundred and nineteen pounds," says the nurse, looking at the scale. I'm not completely surprised to learn I've lost weight. The uncomfortable feeling in my throat has made it difficult for me to swallow and I often opt out of meals.

Dr. Sparks sends me for a full medical workup. Blood work is ordered; I'm given an endoscopy to make sure I don't have polyps or cancer. After being told there is nothing physically wrong with me, I work with a voice therapist who tells me I am a "vocal over-doer" and gives me exercises to manage my volume and calm my vocal folds, but nothing alleviates the uncomfortable fullness in my throat.

"There are medications that can help with this," Dr. Sparks says. He knows I've had sensitivities to different medications in the past – lidocaine and tetracycline, as well as the three different anti-depressants I tried under his care -- and I trust his medical opinion.

When I ask about possible side effects, he doesn't mention a single one. "It's a baby dose," he says. "Plus, it's a drug that's been around since the 1950's. It's tried and true."

Having suffered years of chronic throat pain and insomnia, I'm willing to try anything, and on March 2, 2004, Dr. Sparks writes me a thirty-day prescription for 0.5 milligrams of clonazepam. "Take half a pill at bedtime," he says.

After my appointment, I drive straight to the nearest grocery store, and as I complete the weekly shopping for my family, a pharmacist fills a little brown bottle with dozens of tiny pills. Outside of what is written on the bottle, I'm given no information about my new medication at all. And because we have excellent insurance, I pay only five dollars for my first prescription, less than the cost of a Big Mac Meal at McDonald's.

It seems like a good deal.

That night, I take my medication exactly as prescribed, and for the first time in years, I fall asleep within fifteen minutes of getting into bed. I sleep the entire night and, in the morning, I wake feeling refreshed and energized. "That clonazepam is a miracle!" I tell my husband, as he heads off to work.

While he is away, I find myself feeling energetic and extremely focused. I'm able to read for hours, and my writing feels sharp and fresh. I feel excited about this new medication that is going to help me get my life back on track.

It is often said that if something seems too good to be true, it probably is.

And while I didn't know it at the time, that first bit of clonazepam was as far away from a miracle as they come.

It was a deal with the devil.

CHAPTER 5

FALLING APART

For the next nine months, I take clonazepam at bedtime, exactly as my primary care physician prescribes. My husband comes from a medical family, and everyone has a lot of faith in pharmaceuticals. They've been hearing about my insomnia for years, and they're relieved that I'm sleeping again and feeling well enough to take a long-anticipated vacation with our son.

A month before the trip our trip to Florida, I notice that the extreme focus I'd been feeling has been inexplicably replaced by a feeling of sedation, especially in the mornings. I attribute this side effect to the clonazepam, and I call my doctor to ask him what I should do.

"Cut it in half," he says. "Wait a week and then cut it in half again. It'll be a tiny little crumb, and by the time you go to Florida, you shouldn't even need it anymore."

I follow my primary care physician's "tapering" instructions, and a few days before our trip to Florida, I stop the clonazepam completely. What I didn't realize at the time – and what many prescribing doctors still don't seem to understand -- is that benzodiazepines should never be stopped abruptly. Weaning off benzodiazepines can take years, and people who quit them without a slow, careful taper may experience life-threatening grand mal seizures. They may also experience delirium and hallucinations that can cause a loss with reality.

When Derek, Cal and I board the airplane in Rochester on our way to Florida a few days after I abruptly stopped the clonazepam, I feel well enough. But after our first full day at The Magic Kingdom, I find that I can't sleep at all, and as I stare at the digital clock, its red numbers illuminating the darkness, I attribute the bout of insomnia to the travel, the strange hotel room, and my excitement about the trip.

After a night without sleep, I feel jittery and agitated. We go to Animal Kingdom where my husband repeatedly tells me I'm walking too fast, that Cal can't keep up. And while I want to slow down, I can't. I need to keep moving. When I sit still, my legs shake involuntarily.

If a person is going to have a manic episode, Disney World is a pretty good place to have one. People don't look at you. There are a million attractions, there are people in costumes and parades and concerts and stunt-shows and rides on which you can twirl and whirl and go round and round. There are princesses wearing pink and purple tulle and everyone has mouse-ears. With all that is going on around you, you simply can't look as crazy as you feel.

At one point, while I'm watching Cal enjoy himself on a playground, I distinctly hear a woman's voice. *Die*, she says. It's just a whisper, but it's vivid enough to make me look around and see if I've actually heard a piece of conversation or if I've heard something meant just for me, a secret message delivered directly to my ears.

That night, I can't sleep again, and instead of bothering my husband, I decide to go outside. The mosquitoes are out, and I feel them devouring me. Slipping into the pool, I swim several dozen laps hoping to wear myself out, and while my body is exhausted, my brain won't let me rest.

On my way back to the hotel room, I find an enclosed laundry area and sit down on the cement floor. *You are a terrible person*, the voice insists. These days, it is fairly well known that psychotropic drugs can cause suicidal ideation, but at the time, I had no idea what was happening to me. No one had articulated a correlation between psychiatric medications and suicidal thoughts and the condition wasn't listed in any of the informational inserts I had received. That night, I spend a good part of the night crying in that laundry room, finding dark symbolism in the labels on different detergents. Feeling a little like Alice lost in Wonderland, I notice an abandoned bottle of bleach resting sideways on a shelf.

Drink me, a voice says.

Sitting there alone in a pile of gray lint, I am awash in self-hatred. It takes all my willpower not to hurt myself that night. I've never been suicidal before, and I'm scared of the thoughts I'm having. I return to my hotel room a little while later and slide into bed for yet another sleepless night.

It's only in hindsight that I now recognize what I was experiencing is the onset of benzodiazepine withdrawal. After nine months on the drug, I am chemically dependent on clonazepam. Short-acting drugs like alprazolam (Xanax) and lorazepam (Ativan) leave the system quickly, which means withdrawal symptoms can appear in as little as 8 to 12 hours, while longer-acting benzos like diazepam (Valium) and clonazepam (Klonopin) can stay in the system longer, which means it can be several days before withdrawal symptoms start. [6]

After four full days in Disney theme parks and three nights without sleep, I am feeling generally unwell. Alternating between shivering and sweating, I don't realize that the physical symptoms I'm experiencing are due to the abrupt cessation of the clonazepam. After all, a doctor helped me to get off of the drug, and I followed his directions to the letter. I assume, instead, that I have caught some kind of virus or that, perhaps, I am beginning to experience early menopause.

Though I try to put on a happy face for the sake of my husband and son, even Cal - now six-years old – notices "mommy is acting funny," alternately hippie-dippy high happy and then desperately, inconsolably sad.

That night, after we put our son to bed, I motion for Derek to join me outside in the hallway. Sobbing into my hands, I confess I haven't slept a wink since we arrived in Florida, that the insomnia is back, and that I'm having suicidal thoughts, too. "I need something to slow down my brain," I sob.

From a thousand miles away, Derek calls Dr. Sparks back in Rochester, New York to ask him if he can send a refill prescription for clonazepam to a nearby Florida pharmacy. Dr. Sparks informs Derek that he will do his best, but that filling prescriptions out of state is a complicated procedure. An hour later, Dr. Sparks calls back to inform Derek that he has completed the necessary paperwork and submitted it to a nearby pharmacy via fax – in triplicate.

It's late when Derek leaves the hotel room with the keys to the rental car. He's not sure where he is going or if the pharmacy will still be open when he gets there. While he is gone, I sit on the floor with my head in my hands. A little while later, Derek returns with exactly three pills.

"That's it?" I ask, looking inside the bottle in my hand.

"Apparently, that's all he could write for," Derek says. "Not to mention our out-of-state insurance wasn't accepted so I had to pay out of pocket. You're looking at sixty dollars right there."

"Three pills cost sixty dollars?!" I ask incredulously.

"Yup," Derek says. "You're going to have to make it last."

At the time, none of this registers with me, but I now understand the reason Dr. Sparks had to work so hard to get a pharmacy to fill my prescription: clonazepam is a controlled substance.

I reinstate the clonazepam while I am in Florida, grateful to get some much-needed sleep. But with only two extra pills and three extra days of vacation, it doesn't take long before I begin to experience withdrawal symptoms again.

The plane ride back to Rochester is horrendous; it's impossible for me to sit still. Wringing my hands, I cross and uncross my legs the whole way home. I'm certain I look like someone who should be in a straightjacket. It's difficult for me to believe that people don't notice my shaking, but Derek reassures me that on the outside, I look fine.

After what feels like forever, the three of us finally make it back to our house in suburbia. I carry Cal upstairs and settle him into his bed, and then I go into the bathroom and find my bottle of clonazepam. I quickly cut one of my pills in half and swallow it down without any water. I know Derek is bringing in the suitcases, and I go downstairs to help him. As I walk down the long hall, Derek comes in from the garage carrying the last bag and drops his keys onto the bench in our mudroom. "We can't continue like this," he says. "We've got to get you some help."

CHAPTER 6
DIAGNOSIS

The day after we return from Orlando, I make an appointment for myself with a psychiatrist whose name I pull out of the phonebook, and a few days later, I find myself in Dr. Sypher's office.

Dr. Sypher is a tall, smug man. With his long legs crossed, he sits in a tiny chair in the far right-hand corner of his office. Within fifteen minutes of our initial meeting, he diagnoses me with Bipolar II (NOS). "It's obvious that you have a combination of anxiety, depression and Bipolar II," Dr. Sypher says. "It's simply a matter of trial and error until we find the right combination of drugs." From out of a discombobulated file drawer, he pulls a photocopied pamphlet of information along with a dosing schedule. "Lamictal can cause a serious skin condition resulting in a blistering, bloody mess," Dr. Sypher says. "If you experience a rash accompanied by a fever, stop the medication immediately and get to an emergency room."

Everything seems to be happening very quickly, and I feel uncertain. When I tell Dr. Sypher that .25 milligrams of clonazepam isn't helping me to sleep anymore, he hands me a new prescription. "I'm bumping up your dose a little bit," he says.

When I tell Dr. Sypher about how I'd felt sedated on the clonazepam, which was why I'd stopped it, he shakes his head. "It's my job to help you find the right cocktail of drugs to balance your brain," he says. "If you had diabetes, and I told you to take insulin, would you challenge me about the treatment?"

“I don’t know,” I say. “I might want to get a second opinion.”

Dr. Sypher crosses his arms over his chest defensively. “If you don’t want my help, why did you come here?” Standing up from his chair, he towers over me and walks toward the door. Suddenly, I find myself trying to placate the doctor. I don’t want him to walk out on me.

“So, you want me to take both of these medications?” I ask.

“They work best together,” Dr. Sypher says. “Fill the prescriptions and make a follow-up appointment with the receptionist,” he says.

And because I’m a good patient, I do exactly as I am told.

In the parking lot outside the doctor’s office, I sit in my car and stare at the tiny slip of paper in my hand. I read the pamphlet Dr. Sypher has given me on Bipolar Disorder, and I am positively terrified. I don’t know what any of the terms mean and I have to keep referring back to a little glossary, which defines words like “mania” and “hypomania,” and other words like “delusion” and “hallucination.”

I read that Lamictal has been recently approved for treatment of Bipolar Affective Disorder, and that it is the first general treatment since Lithium was approved thirty years earlier. According to the pamphlet, Lamictal was originally marketed as an anti-seizure medication for epilepsy. From what I can tell, Lamictal has fewer side effects than Lithium, which can damage the kidneys.

While many people may feel a sense of relief in being given a diagnosis and readily accept the medications they are given, I don't feel good about taking drugs, but years of chronic insomnia have worn me down.

Now, in addition to a nightly dose of clonazepam, I add Lamictal to my "treatment plan" and slowly titrate up from 12.5 milligrams to 50 milligrams, about 1/3 of what is typically considered a "therapeutic" dose. And while I don't get the dreaded Steven-Johnson Rash that Dr. Sypher warned me about, I do experience many unpleasant side effects, including itchy hands and feet, a dry mouth, and severe lower back pain which makes me feel as though someone has hit me with a truck in the middle of the night and then returned me to my bed.

Dr. Sypher had mentioned it could take several weeks or even months for my body to get used to the medication, and because I want the Lamictal to work, I continue to soldier through the uncomfortable side effects. All I want is to get well. I want to be a good wife and a good mother. I don't want to cry all the time; I just want my throat to stop hurting and to be able to get some reliable sleep.

About six months into my new medication protocol, my hair begins to fall out in clumps. Rather than immediately question the doctor, I purchase hair extensions and start wearing hats. When I tell Dr. Sypher what's happening at one of our monthly "med checks," he consults his pamphlet. "Hair loss is not a recognized side effect of Lamictal," he says. "Luckily, trichotillomania can be treated effectively with clonazepam," Dr. Sypher says, writing me a new script.

"I'm not pulling out my hair," I insist. "It's just coming out."

"You mean, you're not pulling it out *intentionally*," Dr. Sypher says.

"No," I say. "I'm not pulling it out at all. It's just… falling out." As I try to further explain my situation, I detect something in this doctor, something akin to disdain. Dr. Sypher scrunches up his nose, making the kind of face a child might make if he smelled something foul. "Don't you believe me?" I ask.

In her book *Within Our Reach: Ending the Mental Health Crisis*, former first lady Rosalynn Carter describes stigma, a strong feeling of disgrace, as "the most damaging factor in the life of anyone who has a mental illness. It humiliates and embarrasses; it is painful; it generates stereotypes, fear and rejection; it leads to terrible discrimination." And it is in Dr. Sypher's office that I first feel the stigma associated with being diagnosed with a mental illness. Suddenly, I am no longer trusted to be a credible source even about my own feelings. If my own doctor – an expert in the mental health profession -- doubts my ability to perceive and accurately report about my life experience, then it seems reasonable that other people might begin to view me negatively too.

When I confide in my family about what's going on, my father-in-law insists that I should keep my diagnoses to myself, and my sense of shame leads me to secret keeping. I am never given an opportunity to talk about what brought me to the medication in the first place – the trauma surrounding the labor and delivery of my son and my subsequent feelings of grief and fear associated with the NDE, the disconnection between my husband and myself – and now I question my knowledge about myself and my own needs. Suddenly, every conversation is about the medication. Am I up or am I down? Manic or depressed?

After many years of being part of the mental health system, I've become accustomed to be being spoken to as if I am a second-class citizen. Having learned to stifle my feelings and thoughts so as not to inconvenience others, I now give over my power to someone who I'm told knows more than I do and, ostensibly, knows better.

• • •

In 2006, I begin to experience constant urinary tract infections, kidney infections, intense muscle cramping, skin problems, and a host of other troubling medical ailments. Dr. Sparks wants to rule out his concern that my issues could be physiological in nature, and – once again -- I have a complete physical, donate vials of blood and cups of urine to rule out anything serious.

All the tests come back normal.

Despite the fact that every doctor I see asks me to report every medication I am taking – which I do – not one medical professional ever suggests that the psychiatric drugs I am taking could be causing my physical symptoms. And even though I experience a decline in my physical wellness, I remain a compliant patient and continue to take my medications exactly as prescribed.

On a monthly basis, Dr. Sypher reminds me that I am, in fact, bipolar and in need of medication, probably for life. In an attempt to accept this fact, I find an online support group for people who have been diagnosed with bipolar disorder, but the more I research, the more I believe I have not been diagnosed properly. After all, I've never been unable to work. I've always been productive and completion-oriented. I've never had legal problems. Folks with bipolar disorder tend to lack impulse control; they often go on spending sprees or recklessly gamble away their money, but I've always been fiscally responsible. If anything, I tend to be frugal. I don't get into fights with people. Could I be moody, absolutely, yes – but out and out brawls? Never.

I begin to question my diagnosis, but how do you to clean up a mess that you can't see, can't test for, and might not really be there at all?

CHAPTER 7
NUMB

One afternoon, Derek walks through the door after a particularly long day at the office. As I look up from my cutting board where I've been slicing apples, he barely acknowledges me; instead, he heads upstairs to change his clothes – and while I feel slighted, I don't say anything.

Long before I ever began looking for pharmacological solutions to my problems, I wrestled with the fact that my husband and I have been drifting apart. Now, when Derek comes home after work, he busies himself in activities with our son and tackles a host of household chores, which I appreciate, but the disconnection between the two of us is especially obvious in the bedroom.

I've always had a strong libido, but with the introduction of the clonazepam, my desire goes completely down the tubes. It is a well-documented fact that many psychotropic drugs lower the libido in both men and women, and benzodiazepines act like alcohol in that they overwhelm the individuals' neurotransmitters, causing people to black out.

Over the last fifteen years, a number of high-profile date rape cases involved sexual predators using the benzodiazepine flunitrazepam to sedate and control their victims. Commonly referred to as Rohypnol or "Rufies," when ingested, flunitrazepam causes individuals to black out, making it impossible for victims to defend themselves and, because of its impact on the memory, victims are often not able to remember the details surrounding what has happened to them.

If someone had informed me that by taking clonazepam every night for sleep that I was essentially drinking an entire bottle of alcohol with the intention to black out, I'm not sure that I would have agreed to do that. But at this time, I believe that my medications are safe because a doctor is prescribing them to me. Each night, I dutifully take my pills, and within fifteen minutes, I'm sound asleep.

I assume Derek is as upset as I am about what isn't happening in our bedroom, but we no longer discuss this issue at all. In my medicated state, I am unaware of how zombified I truly am. In truth, nothing much matters to me. The combination of Lamictal and clonazepam dial my intensity down so much that I no longer feel compelled to do the laundry, make the beds, or go to the grocery store. I feel fuzzyheaded. Because clonazepam has a slight amnesic effect, I sometimes have trouble remembering details. When I sit down to type and then look up at the screen, the letters appear scrambled, and I am finding I have to concentrate very hard to do things that once came easily.

I try to believe the medications are helping me: that my shattered pieces are recovering and being super-glued firmly back into place. I try to believe it, but it is another lie.

CHAPTER 8
SECOND OPINION

Though Dr. Sypher is adamant that I am suffering from a serious mental illness that will require medication for life, I decide to seek another opinion, this time from a female psychiatrist.

Dr. Borowitz works at a busy clinic in a lower-income suburb of the city. Ten or twelve psychiatrists work in this clinic where the waiting room is huge, and dozens of patients come and go every few minutes. Tan and thin, Dr. Borowitz administers the same mental health questionnaire that I was given at Dr. Sypher's office, and she immediately agrees that I am, in fact, bipolar. She is more than happy to write me scripts for clonazepam, she says, and see me every month, on the condition that I begin working with a therapist within the clinic's practice. This is the first time anyone has suggested I might benefit from talk therapy.

For so long, I've wanted to talk to someone about what is happening with my marriage, the lack of intimacy between my husband and me. With the addition of weekly visits to Shelby, my new therapist, I am now spending $300 a month on talk-therapy and medications. Derek doesn't seem to mind the expense, and I definitely enjoy my time with Shelby.

Young and pretty, Shelby and I relate to each other in an easy, friendly manner. At my weekly appointments, we sit in close proximity to one another, and she leans in to listen to me when I speak. If I say something funny, she laughs. If I say something serious, she looks at me intently. I appreciate Shelby's attentiveness, and she is happy to listen to me rehash all kinds of events that have transpired in my life, but none of this talking feels particularly productive to me. When I talk to her about the lack of intimacy between my husband and myself, she assures me that there are sexual ebbs and flows within every marriage and that these rhythms are further exacerbated by the arrival of children. “You just need to be patient with him,” Shelby says. “I’m sure he’ll eventually come around.”

One year later, Dr. Borowitz informs me that she is changing her practice so she can focus exclusively on the needs of pediatric psychiatric patients. She tells me that she won’t be able to see me anymore as a patient, and because she can’t see me anymore, Shelby can’t work with me anymore either.

The idea of starting over with a new psychiatrist and a new therapist is overwhelming. Something inside of me coils up like a rattlesnake, and I’m furious at what feels like abandonment by my mental health team. When I press Dr. Borowitz for names of new providers, she can offer none and simply shrugs her skinny tan shoulders.

Odd as it sounds, I’m devastated. Traveling to the other side of the city provides me with some kind of delusional sense of superiority that I am better off than the most of patients at the downtown office. Over the months, I’ve gotten used to sitting in the waiting room next to the women who mumble to themselves in languages I cannot understand; I know my way through the maze of hallways connecting offices filled with health care providers. Unlike most of the patients at the city clinic who arrive via public transportation, I own my own car and drive myself to my appointments. I don’t stand outside the electronic glass doors in the freeze of winter smoking because I need something to fill the void.

I don’t have those problems, I smugly think to myself. *I’m not as sick as they are.*

It will be years before I realize that the only difference between the patients at the clinic and me is that I haven't been on the drugs as long as they have.

CHAPTER 9

YET ANOTHER OPINION

With prescription medication that will soon need to be refilled, I feel pressure to find another doctor, and this time I find someone on my side of town.

As it turns out, Dr. Solomon is able to provide psychotherapy as well as prescription medication, and his streamlined approach immediately feels fifty percent less cumbersome than having to fit two appointments with two different practitioners into my schedule. He impresses me by getting me in for an appointment right away, and this convenience makes me overlook the fact that his office waiting room is completely cosmetically outdated. The walls are plastered in metallic wallpaper, and four very stiff metal chairs, upholstered in mauve, encircle a small oval table upon which a few old magazines have been carefully arranged into a fan configuration. A single plastic plant stands upright in one corner of the room, and while I am waiting to see the doctor for my first visit, the secretary comes out to dust the faux-leaves with a damp cloth.

Dr. Solomon is a one-man operation and he matches his office to a tee. Short and stocky with graying hair and beard, he looks like he has stepped out of the Sears catalogue circa 1957. Wearing polyester dress pants, an Oxford button up shirt, and a wide striped tie, Dr. Solomon meets me in the waiting room, takes me by the hand, and escorts me back to his office where he goes to sit behind a mammoth-sized wood desk strewn with papers and books. I take a seat in a chair across from him on the other side of the desk.

When I start to tell him about my diagnoses, he holds up one hand to signal me to stop talking. "Now just hold it right there," he says. "I'm an old-fashioned kind of doc. I want to figure out what's been troubling you myself. I don't want to have my ideas colored by anyone else's. So, if you don't mind," he continues, "... just leave the diagnosis out and we'll take it from there."

"But I have medications that are going to need to be filled," I protest. "Aren't you going to figure out the issue based on the medication?"

"I'll know what your last person thought would help," he says. "Right now, I want to hear how you feel."

I like that Dr. Solomon is a questioner of authority. I appreciate that he isn't just going to concur and that he is going to take his time and figure things out by himself. By our fourth or fifth hour-long session, Dr. Solomon tells me he'd like to wean me off the Lamictal to see what happens.

It is 2007 now, and I have been completely psychiatrized. At this point, I believe I am a deeply flawed individual with a chemical deficiency. Therapy has confirmed that I am impatient and aggressive, too extroverted, too emotional, and too talkative.

"Won't I get all manic and crazy?" I ask. The idea of stopping the medication that I have been assured I need for emotional stability is frightening.

"I don't think so," Dr. Solomon says. "I think you're anxious, but I don't think you're bipolar."

Dr. Solomon instructs me about how to stop taking the Lamictal. “You’re on such a tiny dose,” he says. “I don’t think you’ll have any trouble stopping it, but let’s take it slow.” Over a month-long period, I wean off of 25 milligrams of Lamictal. While many people report intense mood swings coming off Lamictal, I do not experience this; however, I do experience the onset of migraine headaches that debilitate me for a period of several months. A private neurologist prescribes Topamax, and by Thanksgiving the headaches ease up and my hair grows back.

Much later, I learn that coming off Lamictal too quickly can cause intense headaches, but at the time, I’m grateful to Dr. Solomon for recommending that I stop the Lamictal and due to this success, my trust in him increases.

For the next four years, I see Dr. Solomon every three months during which time he offers me his version of psychotherapy. When I talk to him about my marital problems that have been going on now for over a decade, he showers me with compliments: “You have a beautiful face and figure,” he says. “If I were your husband, we would rarely leave the house.” During the course of my life, I have received similar kinds of comments from male school teachers, members of the clergy, construction workers, and even spouses of friends, and I handle Dr. Solomon’s attentions in much the same way I’ve handled them in the past, which is to say I deflect them politely.

At the end of each appointment, Dr. Solomon writes my prescription for clonazepam – between 120 and 240 pills at a time -- and, once in a while, if I forget to remind him about needing a new prescription, he has his secretary pop one in the mail for me to save me the inconvenience of having to make a trip to his office.

This is the second time my body has adapted to the medication I am being prescribed. The first time this occurred, Dr. Sypher upped my dose from .25 milligrams to .50 milligrams. And now Dr. Solomon increases my dose to 1 milligram at bedtime. Though no one explains this to me at the time, what I am experiencing is a phenomenon called tolerance or dependence. When a person reaches tolerance, it means the drug they are taking loses its efficacy, so that it no longer addresses the original symptoms it was prescribed to treat. At the same time, the patient begins to complain about new and worsening symptoms, and it is typical for the doctor to then prescribe higher and more frequent dosing to achieve the same initial effects.

When I reach tolerance, my insomnia returns – so whenever I experience a series of three or more sleepless nights, Dr. Solomon simply increases my clonazepam dose. It doesn't seem like a big deal; in fact, many people insist that I'm taking only a "baby dose" of medication. My own husband confirms that he sees patients' charts with people reporting that they regularly take eight or ten milligrams of clonazepam.

Because a doctor is prescribing the drug I am taking and because I am well below anything close to that kind of dose, I develop a false sense of security that the medication I am taking is safe. In reality, clonazepam is about fifteen times stronger than Valium – and during the time that I am Dr. Solomon's patient, my clonazepam dose edges up from 0.50 milligrams daily to 2.25 milligrams daily –a 350% increase over four years.

Strangely, the uptick in my dose doesn't register with me at all. In my mind, clonazepam is harmless: just a little something I take to help me sleep. There certainly don't seem to be any negative consequences for taking it.

One night though, while my husband is out of town, I hire a babysitter to watch our son and I decide to meet a few friends out at a local dance club. While waiting for my girlfriends to consume their cocktails, I drink ice water. Anyone who spends any time with me knows that I've never cared much for the taste or the effects of alcoholic beverages. As a former dancer, I don't need anything to loosen me up: the dance floor is a comfortable space for me, and I feel confident about the way I move to the music. The DJ is playing tunes from the 1970s and 80s, and we're all having a very good time, dancing and laughing, when a wave of sudden dizziness washes over me.

It is if the earth has tipped off its axis, and I find myself holding onto the wall for support. Looking around, I'm overwhelmed with fear. It seems like everyone is laughing at me, and with good reason: there is hardly anything less attractive than an inebriated adult, and I'm aware that I'm stumbling around as if I'm completely intoxicated. Retreating to a pub table in the corner, I plan to sit and wait for my head to clear.

Except it doesn't.

The world is spinning faster and faster, and I begin to worry that someone may have slipped something into my water.

After a while, one of my girlfriends joins me at the table. She can tell something is up with me, and I tell her I'm not feeling well. My friend says she's had enough excitement for the night, and when she offers to drive me home, I take her up on it. It's raining lightly outside, and I lean against my friend for support as we make our way to her car. I apologize repeatedly for causing her to go out of her way, and as my friend's headlights penetrate the darkness, I feel the world surging around me with an uncomfortable pulsating energy. Glancing at the digital clock on the dashboard of the car, I see it's well after midnight – nearly two hours past my normal bedtime, and

I wonder if my extreme dizziness could be the result of being overtired.

Once inside my house, I pay my babysitter and lock the door behind her when she leaves. After climbing the stairs, I tiptoe into Cal's bedroom to look in on my son and to make sure that he is sleeping soundly. After adjusting the comforter on his bed, I turn off the light in his closet and return to the hallway. Our brand new carpet feels soft beneath my feet as I walk down the hall, into the master bedroom, and instead of stopping in front of my dresser to put on my pajamas, I go straight to the master bathroom where I open the drawer to the left of the sink. This is the place I keep my nighttime essentials: toothbrush and toothpaste, nail clippers, pill slicer and medication. I take two white pills out of one bottle and one yellow pill from out of another bottle. Turning on the tap, I wait for the water to get cold before swallowing my pills, one at a time.

Within five minutes, my uncomfortable dizziness completely disappears, and the world stops vibrating.

I take this as proof positive that there is something wrong with me, a chemical imbalance of some sort, something faulty in the way I am wired, a defect for which I will require medication for the rest of my life.

Never for one minute did I ever consider that daily clonazepam use might be harming my brain.

• • •

In August of 2011, I enter the busy office park for my regularly scheduled quarterly med check. Inside, I find Dr. Solomon's office locked, with a handwritten note taped outside the heavy wood door. The note states Dr. Solomon has decided to stop practicing medicine, and patients are instructed to consult with their primary care physicians to be referred to new psychiatric providers.

With only a few days left before I run out of prescription medication and knowing that I am not supposed to miss even a single dose of clonazepam, I immediately call my primary care physician, who asks me to come to his office that same afternoon.

Upon my arrival, Dr. Sparks explains that Dr. Solomon has lost his medical license since the New York State Medical Board has recently found him guilty of professional misconduct regarding improper prescription practice.

"That's terrible," I say. "I wonder what he was prescribing improperly?"

At this point, I am in complete denial that I am, in fact, one of the many patients who have been harmed by Dr. Solomon's unethical prescription practices. Because I have excellent medical insurance, I regularly see a primary care physician, a gynecologist, a neurologist, and a dentist: each of whom collects a full report of any and all medications I might be taking; yet, no one ever raises an eyebrow regarding my long-term clonazepam use. My own husband, a medical doctor, repeatedly reassures me that he sees numerous patients every day who take nearly ten times the dose I take. Because everyone has always been so casual about my clonazepam use, I'm completely unaware of the dangers associated with this class of drug.

"Will you be able to refill my prescription this month?" I ask Dr. Sparks; after all he was the doctor who first offered me the script.

"I can't prescribe that drug for you," he says, looking sad and stern.

"Why not?" I ask.

"Benzodiazepines are highly habit-forming," Dr. Sparks says. "They are a controlled substance. After taking them for this long, you've undoubtedly developed a chemical dependency. You're going to need an addiction specialist."

"An addiction specialist?!" I say. "For what?!"

"To help you wean off this drug safely."

With the word "addiction" rolling around inside my head, I consider my notion of what a drug addict would look like. At this point in my life, I've seen dozens of movies about people who got caught up in illegal drugs. In every case, addicts were shifty, lazy, dirty -- and toothless. They lied, cheated and stole to get money for their next fix. They were often depicted as deeply flawed individuals, born without a moral compass and lacking in self-control.

"I've never taken more than Dr. Solomon prescribed," I say, shaking my head.

"I know," Dr. Sparks says, shaking his head. "Unfortunately, it doesn't matter."

Now I'm thoroughly confused. In my quest for better living through pharmaceuticals, I've spent most of my 30s -- nearly a decade -- snowed.

At this time in my life, I know nothing about physiological or chemical dependencies. The last time I heard the word 'dependency,' I was in 12th grade, studying the effects of cocaine and heroin in health class. Like many people before me, I'm operating under a misguided belief that because licensed medical doctors have been managing my medications, I'm somehow exempt from experiencing the kinds of complications that a street addict might experience when coming off their drug-of-choice.

I will soon learn otherwise.

CHAPTER 10 WEAN

My addiction specialist turns out to be a petite woman with long dark hair. Always well-dressed and wearing fabulous shoes, Dr. Patricia Halligan, with her impeccable sense of fashion, reassures me that she knows what she's doing. Located on the second floor of a fancy medical building, Dr. Halligan's psychiatry office is a cozy space with off-white walls, expensive-looking artwork, and huge picture windows, which allows patients to enjoy the birds flitting to and from well-stocked bird feeders.

It is in this office where I first begin to understand the severity of my situation. Dr. Halligan tells me that benzodiazepines are associated with all kinds of long-term health problems. "You're young and pretty and smart," she says. "Let's get you off these meds."

Dr. Halligan recommends that I begin working with a new therapist before I start weaning off the clonazepam, and I am fortunate to land in the practice of Vickijo Campanaro -- a warm, supportive and competent practitioner who is proficient in Eye Movement Desensitization and Reprocessing (EMDR). Developed in 1987 for the treatment of post-traumatic stress disorder (PTSD), EMDR is an individual therapy intended to change the way traumatic memories are stored in the brain.

Since this is not my first time working with a therapist, Vickijo and I get into the thick of things rather quickly. I explain to her my thoughts and emotions around early messaging that I received in my family of origin, and from my peers, my school, my religion, and the dominant culture. We look at several significant traumas that occurred in my life before the age of seventeen, including a home invasion, several incidents of sexual assault, as well as a rape. We also explore the betrayal I felt after learning of the infidelity of my first romantic partner and the subsequent dissolution of our relationship. I confess to being emotionally devastated after each of these life events, and talking about them makes me feel like I am reliving them. With Vickijo's help, I am finally able to confront difficult thoughts and memories associated with each of these traumatic events, and she assists me in connecting with corrective information for maladaptive, unrealistic or problematic thoughts that drive post-traumatic stress symptoms.

When we begin to talk about the lack of physical and emotional intimacy in my marriage, Vickijo makes a connection between the events of my early life and the man that I chose to marry. "You married someone safe," she says. "Subconsciously, some part of you knew that he was kind and that he would never pressure you or make you feel overwhelmed sexually. You had a strong friendship and you trusted that he would never cheat on you, but the chemistry isn't there."

Vickijo's words resonate with me on some levels, but not on others. "I'm attracted to my husband," I tell her. "I don't think that is the issue." At some point, Vickijo suggests that my husband might benefit from individual therapy, but when I mention her recommendation to Derek, he insists that he doesn't need or want therapy.

"But if you think it's helping you," he says, "then go for it."

• • •

Beginning in October 2012, with Vickijo's support and Dr. Halligan's guidance, I agree to taper from 2.5 milligrams of clonazepam daily to 0.25 milligrams over a seven-month period. When I can't reliably make cuts by hand anymore, Dr. Halligan tells me she will switch me over to an equivalent dose of Valium (diazepam) so I can continue to wean.

Dr. Halligan reassures me that I won't have any trouble. "You might gain a little weight," she says. "Sometimes people start to crave sweets as they come off benzos."

During my entire taper, Dr. Halligan allows me to go at my own pace and encourages me to listen to my body, which I appreciate. I meet with her monthly, following to the letter her notes regarding how to withdraw properly from the drug.

Discontinuing psychiatric medication is complicated since everyone's body responds differently to the process. Because many medical professionals doubt the reality of a persistent discontinuation syndrome associated with the cessation of psychiatric drugs, there have not been any studies devoted to studying how stopping mood-altering drugs might affect the brain. As a result, there are no accurate statistics regarding how many people are negatively impacted when trying to discontinue psychiatric medications. It has been estimated, though, that 25% of people seem to be able to wean off their psychiatric medications with relative ease; 50% of people seem to experience moderate to severe symptoms that last between 6 months and a year; and 25% of people seem to experience extended, debilitating symptoms which may last for over two years and can be life-threatening.[7]

During my taper, I stay on a reliable schedule and carefully reduce my dose every two weeks. Each time I make a cut, I hold the new dose for two weeks before making the next reduction. Luckily, I experience only mild side effects, mainly increased insomnia and fatigue.

Though Derek is aware of my taper schedule, I handle the reductions on my own. At this point in our marriage, our conversations are mainly limited to discussions about our son and where I am in my taper. Outside of that, our interactions are businesslike and fairly generic.

During a regular office visit in June of 2013, Dr. Halligan informs me she will be traveling to Europe for the entire month of August. "You're getting close to the end of your taper," she says, "I want to make sure you understand how to handle things while I'm away." It is at this point that Dr. Halligan writes me a new prescription for 5mg/5mL diazepam solution and tells me that I will need to go to a compounding pharmacy to fill the prescription, and she scribbles the name of a place that is not too far away from my house. "I'm switching you over to water titration now," Dr. Halligan continues, explaining that the pharmacy will mix my pill with water to allow me to continue to slowly reduce my dose every day, instead of cutting pills every two weeks. "This method allows the body to adjust to the reductions in a very subtle and gentle way and allows you to have greater control over the rate of your taper," she says.

Because my symptoms have been relatively mild, I'm not at all concerned that Dr. Halligan is going out of the country, and I feel confident that I understand the weaning protocol, which she has written out for me, ending on July 23, 2013.

After leaving Dr. Halligan's office, I fill the new prescription, and in the middle of July, during an impromptu trip to Sarasota, Florida, I take what I believe is my last capsule filled with less than 1 milligram of Valium. After ten months of weaning, I believe I have successfully tapered off the drug, and I splurge on a fancy new dress to celebrate.

For a few days, I don't feel anything.

Then, late one afternoon a weird dizziness sneaks up on me. Derek attributes the onset of my vertigo to turbulence that we experienced on the airplane on our way down to Florida. It sounds reasonable and, over the years I've learned not to question his medical opinions. A few days later, though, I meet a friend for lunch in Sarasota and, inexplicably, I find myself unable to remember her name. Nauseous and shaky, I excuse myself to go to the bathroom and I get lost on the way back to our table from the restroom.

I know something is not right.

When Derek and I return from Florida, I'm still not feeling well, and a quick trip to the gynecologist confirms that I have contracted yet another urinary tract infection. This time, my doctor gives me a prescription for Cipro, a commonly prescribed fluoroquinolone antibiotic that I am supposed to take twice a day for five days.

During this time (and unbeknownst to me), fluoroquinolone antibiotics have become the subject of thousands of lawsuits against manufacturers. In 2008, the FDA begins to require "black box warnings" for fluoroquinolones to acknowledge that this class of drugs can increase patients' risks for tendinitis and tendon rupture. These warnings are the strictest labeling requirements that the Food and Drug Administration (FDA) can mandate for prescription drugs, and they highlight serious and sometimes life-threatening adverse drug reactions associated with prescription drug products.

In 2011, a second boxed warning was added to flouroquinolone antibiotic labels related to an increased risk of worsening symptoms for patients with myasthenia gravis. When I go to fill the prescription, no one says a word to me about the dangers associated with these drugs – and even if they had, I probably would not have had a second thought about them since I have never had any autoimmune issues or any problems with my tendons.

A few years later, warnings are strengthened about the association of fluoroquinolones with disabling and potentially permanent side effects involving tendons, muscles, joints, nerves, and the central nervous system and fluoroquinolone drug makers are required to provide labels to mention the potential for irreversible nerve damage.

In the summer of 2018, many years in the future, another FDA communication will be released related to the risk for coma due to low blood sugar, and mental health side effects including disturbances in attention, disorientation, agitation, nervousness and memory impairment. And in December 2018, yet another announcement will be made about an increased risk of the aorta rupturing, causing massive bleeding and potentially, death, and members of the benzodiazepine community will begin to realize that exposure to fluoroquinolone antibiotics seems to exacerbate withdrawal symptoms.

In 2013, though, I have no idea a class of antibiotics that also negatively impacts the central nervous system. From the moment I take my first dose of Cipro, I begin to feel worse. Nothing could have prepared me for the onslaught of horrifying symptoms that started ten days after discontinuing my last dose of Valium and two days after my first dose of Cipro.

PART TWO
CHRYSALIS

CHAPTER 11
THE BEGINNING OF THE END

A week after returning from Florida, I'm back in Rochester. It's early in the morning on the first day of August, and from the master bedroom, I can hear my husband in the kitchen, making lunch for himself before heading off to work. The pantry clicks open; the knife drawer slides shut.

Wearing a long t-shirt, I walk downstairs tentatively, my hand pressing against the wall for support. I am jittery, my heart pounds, my teeth chatter, and my body buzzes. The floor feels spongy under my feet, like I'm walking on a trampoline or a pile of pillows.

Inside the kitchen, I stand next to our table, looking out the sliding glass doors that lead to our patio and backyard. The world doesn't seem real. I feel like someone has smeared Vaseline over my eyes. It seems like I am watching a dream scene from a movie unroll before me. "The world has edges," I say.

Derek is running late for work, and he's not looking at me.

"The leaves are too green," I say, wiping my eyes. "Everything is too bright and too loud."

Derek puts something inside the refrigerator and closes the door. Hard. He's tired of my complaints.

"Something's wrong," I tell him.

There's a weird sound in my brain. It's a clicking of some sort; I hear it once, twice. And then it happens. My legs give way beneath me and somehow, I'm on the floor, on my back, looking up at the ceiling.

Derek pounds his fist on the granite countertop. "Don't you think you're being a little dramatic?" he asks, stepping over my body. It's not a question though; it's a statement. I hear his footsteps moving away from me, and he mutters his frustrations under his breath as he walks outside. The garage door buzzes open and closed.

There is a vice-like pressure in my head as I have my first seizure. The clicking in my brain is louder now; it sounds like someone turning the dial on an old-fashioned mechanical thermostat. I cannot think my way out of this. I cannot move.

Staring up at the ceiling from my place on the floor, I think about how everything in my entire life has brought me to this moment, how I was groomed to be quiet and compliant by parents, religious leaders and teachers – how – after years of ignoring complicated trauma, I was taught to swallow all my feelings until, finally, I had to swallow pills to help me keep all my pain at bay.

Hours later, when my husband comes home from work, he finds me crying and curled up in a ball in the family room, just steps away from the place I'd collapsed earlier that morning. Clearly concerned, he pulls me to my feet and helps me to the master bedroom at the top of the stairs. After tucking me into bed, he retreats to the bathroom where I hear him run through his nighttime routine. I can easily picture him standing in front of the giant mirror, brushing and flossing his teeth. With the water running, I hear him cough twice and I imagine him sipping some water out of his cupped hand, as is his habit. When he comes out of the bathroom, his pajamas are draped over his forearm. "I'll sleep in the guest room," he says.

We will never sleep in the same bed again.

CHAPTER 12
CRAZY

When my son was young, I introduced him to one of my favorite books, Maurice Sendak's "In the Night Kitchen." The story features the adventurous Mickey, who stirs from his bed to embark on a strange adventure. Young Mickey falls into cake batter, flies across the sky, and ends up right where he started — safe in his own bed.

I'd always fancied myself to be like Mickey: brave and curious, eager for new experiences, unafraid of where they might lead. But during acute benzodiazepine withdrawal, the world is filled with monsters. Where I once appreciated Sendak's idea of an ever-changing landscape over which one has no control, suddenly that lack of control isn't the least bit fun.

For the next three months, I'm like a snail whose shell has been ripped off its back: utterly unprepared, raw and unprotected. Everything is too much. The world is too bright, too noisy. Hands are too rough. My spine burns. My gums recede. My muscles waste away. I develop memory problems, cognitive issues, emotional issues and gastrointestinal problems – none of which were present before taking the medication.

I document everything I am experiencing in black and white composition notebooks leftover from my days as an English teacher. When I look back at what I wrote during withdrawal, I'm aware my words don't come close to capturing the experience. My symptoms read like a laundry list: nausea, diarrhea, muscle aches, and fatigue. My head pounds and, occasionally, it feels like someone is touching my brain with an electric cattle prod. Television screens pulse with a weird energy that hurts my entire body. It is like I have been wrapped up in an electric fence.

Unable to sit still, I rock involuntarily for hours. Unrelenting bladder spasms force me to the restroom dozens of times each hour, even in the middle of the night. Whenever I try to sleep, a continuous ringing in my ears bothers me. I hear invisible doors slamming or the sound of invisible trains. Sometimes I drift off, only to jolt awake a few moments later having had a nightmare.

As if the physical pain caused by stopping the medication is not enough, the psychological symptoms triggered by the withdrawal are doubly terrifying. Suddenly, odd fears I've never had before bubble to the surface. And while part of me is aware that my fears are irrational, I'm powerless over them.

I've always been a social person, comfortable speaking and dancing and generally carrying on in front of large groups of people, but suddenly, I am certain everyone is not only looking at me, they want to harm me. As a result, I develop paralyzing agoraphobia, and I am unable to leave the house.

Everything I put in my mouth has a weird metallic taste or smells like cigarettes; as a result, I develop a fear of food. I lose weight – over twenty pounds in one month -- and become dehydrated.

After a month without any sleep at all, I am completely psychotic. While the rest of the world is still, I sit up alone all night in the basement, crying and praying. One warm September night, I decide I can't take it anymore. I creep upstairs and wake my husband who is fast asleep in the guest bedroom. I tell him I'm afraid of what is happening to me and that I want to die. Derek isn't happy to have been awakened and he convinces me to try some of the pills previous doctors have prescribed.

That night, I have a paradoxical reaction to mirtazapine (Remeron), a commonly prescribed anti-depressant. Much like the horrors in many of my nightmares, I experience a kind of "locked-in" syndrome, where I am awake and aware and yet completely unable to move or sleep. On the outside, I appear to be perfectly still, but on the inside, I am buzzing with electricity. On this particular night, I begin to see things – vivid, nightmarish hallucinations that cause my heart to pound so hard in my chest that I am certain I'm having a heart attack.

There is a man with pointy teeth whose fingers turn into knives. In a prophetic dream, I experience fires and hurricanes, war and plagues and famines. I see my son drown in dark, swirling waters. Each nightmare is darker and more catastrophic than the one that precedes it.

The next day, when the drugs wear off, I call Vickijo, who reassures me that I am on the path to healing, that my neural pathways have to learn basic things again — even things like sleep — after having been dulled for seven years. "It's going to take time," Vickijo always says.

I believe her, and I am prepared to wait it out.

CHAPTER 13
BEDRIDDEN

Somehow it is September again, and the leaves start to fall from the trees. My son is starting 9th grade, and under normal circumstances, I would be the one to handle the back-to-school shopping. But on this day, nothing is anything close to normal.

At this point in my withdrawal, I've had several seizures, which have impacted my brain function, essentially confining me to the master bedroom. Chronic stress affects the production of hormones and the gastro-intestinal system, which can lead to changes in appetite and metabolism. Since I am mostly unable to get downstairs, I'm dependent on Derek to bring me my meals, which he does, once a day at dinnertime. Alone too many hours a day, without enough nutrition, I rapidly lose weight.

One morning, while Derek is at work, I crawl across the room to the corded telephone and call my parents, begging them to pick me up and take me back to their house in Syracuse, ninety miles away from my husband and son. A few hours later, they arrive at my home. My father types our code into the keypad to get into the garage, and I'm relieved when I finally hear his footsteps hurrying up the stairs.

Though he tries to hide his surprise, he is visibly distressed when he sees me. I've always taken great care of my physical appearance, but for several weeks now, I've been suffering from a fear of water, which has made it impossible for me to bathe or shower. Presenting with uncombed hair and an unwashed face, I'm pretty certain I look deranged.

Since I am unable to stand or walk, my father carries me downstairs and outside to the car where my mother is waiting in the front seat. Then he goes back inside to retrieve my plastic laundry basket filled with the few necessary items I've managed to gather together. Besides my purse, a sweater, and a few pairs of yoga pants, I leave everything behind.

On the ride to my parents' house, I lay flat on the backseat, crying and shivering and praying. I'm terrified of being in the car. Driving is impossible, and it is equally awful being a passenger. While my mother and father talk quietly, I feel every bump and swerve. My brain — off the anti-anxiety medication and in acute withdrawal — perceives everything as a threat. Squeezing my eyes shut, all I can do is grip the seat and cry. I'm certain I'm going to die on the ride to Syracuse, and I brace myself for the car accident that I know will end my life.

• • •

I weep with relief when my father pulls into the familiar driveway. Little has changed since I left over twenty-five years earlier; the exterior is still painted gray with white trim; the bushes – generally dense and overgrown – have fused together to become even lumpier and more unkempt. Inside, the same gold couch stretches across the living room; faded curtains cover the windows, and dusty figurines stand at attention on the built-in shelves.

For the first few days, my parents are happy to have me home. My mother runs to the store to buy me clothes and whips up a batch of homemade chicken soup for me. My father rubs my back.

They try to care for me – they do -- but I am stuck in a fear state, my body shaking uncontrollably all the time. Unable to sleep for more than an hour or two each day, I prowl around my parents' house like a caged animal.

Sleep deprivation is often used as a form of torture during times of war, and going without sleep is intensely stressful to one's body and mind. In addition to the insomnia, I am also suffering from visual and auditory hallucinations, and things only get worse once I arrive at my parents' house. I develop new fears. I'm particularly alarmed by the tangled extension cords, which belong to numerous gadgets -- a clock, a fan, a cellphone, a television, a lamp, and I worry about the impending fire, which I am certain will burn us to death.

"How will I escape?" I demand. "The windows are painted shut."

My father tries to convince me that I'm safe, that I'm not going to die.

But fear isn't rational.

One night while my parents are asleep, I roam from room to room, until finally, I unlock the front door and go outside to sit alone in the darkness. The air is thick and hot, and I am the only person outside. I wish for a forest or a desert – someplace I can disappear.

I look up at the moon, full and round and white and I cannot help myself. Beside myself with sadness and fear, I begin to cry, but even my crying sounds strange and unfamiliar. I sound like a wild animal. My sobs are guttural, primitive.

I know why wolves howl at the moon, I think to myself.

Separated from its pack, a wolf uses a lonesome howl, a shortened call that rises in pitch. It is a sound of longing, a desire for connection and a warning signal to others outside the pack to stay away.

And the moon understands.

It doesn't burn the eyes or the skin like the sun does.

I think about how I've always loved summer. How, as a teenager, I waited for the days to unfold like a fan. How, even just one summer prior – while my friends sat in folding chairs in the shade – I'd sprawled out on the newly blacktopped driveway like a weird heat-seeking lizard. I remember how the asphalt used to feel hot against the backs of my legs, how I loved to watch my winter-white skin turn brown.

I remember a time when sleep came easily, how I loved to wake slowly, surrounded by the comfort of warm sheets.

Feeling completely out of control of my body and my mind, I sob with a kind of despair that I have never known before. After a while, I stop crying. The night is warm and the fireflies are out. From somewhere up the street, a dog barks. I decide the time has come for me to do some research, to see what I can find on the Internet.

Maybe I'll be able to find someone else who is going through something like I'm going through now. I think. *Maybe that person will have some advice for me about what to do.*

CHAPTER 14
REALIZATION

The next day, while my parents are out of the house, I use their computer to see if I can figure out what is happening to me. My cognitive abilities wax and wane from day to day. Sometimes, my vision is impaired, making it impossible for me to read. Other times, my vision is clear, but I can't seem to make sense of letters on a page. On this particular morning, I am able to concentrate long enough to research "problems associated with clonazepam" on the Internet, and I am shocked to find entire websites and thousands of threads in chat rooms devoted to the topic of benzodiazepine withdrawal. I quickly connect with a few people who admit they are going through similar experiences. A woman from the Benzo Buddies website asks me if my doctor used the protocol recommended in *The Ashton Manual.*

"*The Ashton Manual*?" I ask. "What's that?"

Written in 1999 and revised in 2002, *The Ashton Manual* is a guide containing information about the effects that benzodiazepines have on the body and the brain. The manual provides detailed instructions about how to withdraw after long-term use as well as individual tapering schedules for different benzodiazepines. Withdrawal symptoms (acute and protracted) are described and suggestions are given about how to cope with them. After downloading a copy of the *Ashton Manual*, I read Dr. Ashton's Revised Forward, written in January 2007:

1. Withdrawal schedules provided in the manual are only intended as general guides. The rate of tapering should never be rigid but

should be flexible and controlled by the patient, not the doctor, according to the patient's individual needs, which are different in every case.

The decision to withdraw is also the patient's decision and should not be forced by the doctor.

2. Note that alcohol acts like benzodiazepines and should be used, if at all, in strict moderation.

3. Antibiotics, for some reason, seem to aggravate withdrawal symptoms. However, one class of antibiotics, the quinolones, actually displace benzodiazepines from their binding sites on GABA-receptors. These can precipitate acute withdrawal in people taking or tapering from benzodiazepines… (and) should be avoided.

After reading this new information, I feel genuinely alarmed. Having recently finished a full course of Cipro, I wonder if the antibiotics have exacerbated my benzo withdrawal. All I know is that I feel I am getting significantly worse every day. I call my psychiatrist's office to inquire about what I should do, and the on-call doctor reminds me that Dr. Halligan is out of the country for another week. "If you think you might hurt yourself, you should go to the Emergency Room," he says.

Somehow, I have enough sense to know that if I go anywhere, I am going to be locked up, possibly restrained and probably poly-drugged with all kinds of psychiatric cocktails. I worry that ER doctors might force me to reinstate the clonazepam I've worked so hard to stop taking, and that thought scares me to death.

I figure I just have to hold on until the withdrawal ends.

It can't last forever, I think to myself.

Later that afternoon, my mother and I have an argument. After returning from the grocery store with a whole organic chicken, she makes a full pot of homemade broth for me, which I tearfully refuse. It isn't that I don't want what she's made – I do! I'm starving! – But I simply can't bring myself to put anything in my mouth. I'm certain that anything I eat will make my symptoms worse. When I try to explain to my mother that I simply can't eat the soup she's made, she crosses her arms over her chest and grits her teeth at me.

"From now on, you can make your own food if you don't like what I make for you," she growls, pushing me toward the open refrigerator where I stand weeping for a long time, trying to decide which foods won't taste like poison. Everything seems dangerous.

After our altercation, I try to calm myself by taking a bath, but my mother barges in on me, unannounced, as I lie naked in the tub. Frightened by my inability to have any kind of personal space, I am filled with panic. Having already left my husband and son in hopes of finding a better place to heal, I realize I've made a mistake in coming to Syracuse. My parents have done the best they can, but I need more than a house with a roof over it in which to heal. I need love and patience and kindness. I need someone to offer encouraging words and tell me I am going to be okay.

Stepping into yoga pants and a t-shirt, I put on my sunglasses and force myself to walk across the street. As my bare feet touch the asphalt, I pray to God that my friend Gina is home.

Gina Wright is the daughter of one of my favorite elementary school teachers, and we have known each other for decades. When she and her husband bought and moved into the house across the street from my parents, I was elated, and whenever I am in town, Gina and I always stop what we are doing to catch up on each other's lives.

It is the end of September and, as I stand on Gina's front stoop, I think about my son eighty miles away: he's started his first year of high school by now, and I know nothing at all about any of his teachers or his classes. As a former educator myself, this is out of character for me, but I know that there is absolutely no way that I take on the role as a responsible mother while I can barely take care of myself.

Tears roll down my cheeks as I ring Gina's doorbell, and a moment later, my old friend pushes open the screen door. I feel certain that Gina must be able to tell that something is very wrong with me, but it seems that she can't. Struck by the chasm between my external appearance and my internal reality, I am bewildered that someone who feels as crazy as I do on the inside wouldn't look the part on the outside.

My hand shakes the entire time we talk. I tell Gina what's going on, that I've weaned off my anti-anxiety medication, and that I am afraid I've lost my mind. Gina listens calmly until I come up for air, then she stands and goes into her kitchen. She returns carrying a phone number scribbled onto a tiny scrap. "There's this new place that offers a bunch of services," Gina says, handing me the paper. "They have a juice bar and a cafe with organic food. Maybe you can give them a call?"

I stay at Gina's house for several hours. Sitting in the safety of my old friend's screened porch, the two of us quietly bead bracelets. Occasionally, we are joined by one of her cats or one of her children – but mostly, it is just the two of us.

Eventually, I return to my parents' gray ranch across the street, and garner enough courage to dial the phone number on the scrap of paper Gina has given me.

It's a phone call that will change my life forever.

CHAPTER 15
NOT MY DAY TO DIE

The phone number Gina gives me is attached to a business, a wellness center offering fresh organic juices and light, healthy meals, vitamin supplements, as well as products sourced from local farms. The woman on the telephone tells me they also offer body services, and before I commit to making an appointment to have a gentle therapeutic massage the following day, I explain to the receptionist that I've recently weaned off a powerful anti-anxiety medication; that I'm in acute withdrawal; and, as a result, extraordinarily sensitive to all sensory stimuli. She assures me that lights will be kept low, and that there will be no music.

Located just five-minutes from my parents' house, my father drives me to the appointment and escorts me inside. I can tell he is terribly worried about me, and he hesitates to leave, saying that he will stay in the waiting room until I'm finished. I insist that he go and do something else, and he reassures me he will pick me up ninety minutes later.

• • •

When the massage therapist opens the door, I'm already lying on my stomach, with my face in the cradle. Theresa introduces herself and asks how I feel about essential oils, and I reluctantly agree to let her use something mild.

I hear rustling sounds, the squeak of a chair, the sound of caps popping open and, after a few moments, three drops of cold liquid land at the center of my back, along my spine.

Instantly, my skin feels like it has been set on fire.

While I might normally be a little self-conscious about being topless in front of a stranger, I sit up on my knees atop the massage table. Theresa is smaller than I'd expected and wearing glasses. "Is that acid?!" I ask her as the burning sensation intensifies. "Did you just pour acid on my back?!"

Theresa double-checks the label on her oil. "It's lavender," she says, turning the bottle towards me as proof.

Tears run down my face, as I beg her to please get it off. She leaves the room and returns with a pail of wet tissues, which she uses to wipe off the oil. Her hands are sandpaper on my skin.

"It's not working!" I sob. "Nothing is working!"

Theresa asks me to be patient. She's certain the burning sensation will subside.

"I want to go home!" I sob, as I slide off the massage table. While I put on my clothes, I think about the concept of home, that place we are supposed to feel comfortable and safe and loved.

For over a year, my husband has listened to my long list of symptoms, eventually opting to spend more time at work and less time with me. And now, back in my hometown, I've overwhelmed my parents with my irrational fears and odd dietary requests. I know that I have them worried. "You should just go back on your medication," my mother has said on more than one occasion.

Back in the tiny treatment room, I squeeze Theresa's hand. "I don't have anywhere to go," I tell her. "Can I stay here? I don't need much." It is a ridiculous question, of course – but at the time, asking to live at the spa seems like a reasonable request.

Theresa apologizes, adding that she wishes she could help me.

After I slip on my shoes, Theresa walks me to the reception area, where I pay full price for services I didn't receive. With nearly an hour to wait before I am to be picked up, I walk outside and find a patch of grass at the entrance to the brick building.

Leaning against the wall, I take in my surroundings. On one level, I know what I am seeing before my eyes is the textbook image of what would normally be considered a "beautiful day." It is warm; the sun is shining; the sky is robin's egg blue; birds chirp and flit from tree to tree. For everyone else in the region, it's the perfect kind of weather for an impromptu bike ride or a trip to the zoo, to tend a garden or take a walk.

But my world is pixelated. My field of vision fluctuates and bends like an image in a distorted mirror. An uncomfortable array of colors and shapes persist behind my closed eyes. My head, body and limbs all feel heavy, as if filled with metal; my hands are cold and without sensation. I have a metallic taste on my tongue; my throat is dry and constricted, and I feel certain I'm suffocating. No matter what I do, no matter what position I try, I simply cannot get comfortable. I feel like my blood has been replaced with battery acid. It is as if I'm being burned alive in a locked room.

I have no idea how long the horrible symptoms will last, and I have no one to talk to about what I'm going through.

It's mid-day, and the road is fairly busy with cars and buses streaming by at a steady pace. It is in this moment that I consider the unthinkable.

What would happen if I step out in front of traffic? I wonder.

From an early age, I am taught that suicide is an abomination to God: that the body belongs to God, and as such, ending one's life is not considered within the scope of a person's authority.

I know what I am thinking is considered a sin, but after living in this terrifying, surreal state of despair for so many months, I can see no other way.

I make a decision.

I will find a way to the roof of the building I am leaning against and dive headfirst onto the pavement. *It will make quite a statement*, I think. *My brain, scrambled by drugs, will literally be scrambled.*

For a moment, I consider my son, how awful it will be to leave him with such a terrible legacy. I don't want to die, but I'm in so much pain, it feels Biblical in its proportion. Nothing anyone has offered me has helped: not my mother's home-cooked meals, not my father's words of encouragement. Unable to escape my symptoms for even a moment, I'm stuck in a nightmare.

You probably have permanent brain damage, a voice whispers in my ear.

"I can't do this anymore," I say aloud.

And then it happens.

A silhouette outlined in white light appears before me, momentarily eclipsing the sun. "Are you okay?" a gentle voice asks.

I wonder if I'm seeing an angel.

"No," I say. I tell the stranger I'm experiencing horrendous withdrawal symptoms after coming off of a medication too abruptly and that I'm planning to jump off the roof of this building in a few minutes.

The woman standing in front of me does not move. With the sun at her back, it appears as though hundreds of white feathers are streaming out of her long dark hair. "Do you have somewhere you can go?" she asks. "Is there someone you can call?"

I shake my head. "Everyone keeps telling me to reinstate the medication, but I just know deep inside it's making me sick."

The woman kneels down beside me. Up close, she looks like Pocahontas, or some other Indian princess. Her skin is glowing in the sun. "Come home with me," she says, putting her hand on my knee. "I'll take care of you for as long as you need. You're going to be okay."

Without so much as a moment's hesitation, I decide I have nothing to lose. I don't care if the dark-haired woman has a torture chamber in her basement, and part of me hopes that if she does, she will kill me quickly. Without asking a single question, I follow her through the parking lot like a stray dog. When she unlocks the doors of her black Expedition, I climb in.

I give the woman directions to my parents' house and, in an instant, we are there. Since I'm not feeling well, I elect to stay in the car and watch a bevy of blackbirds flutter about on Gina's lawn. It's hard for me to imagine the conversation that is happening inside my parents' house, but after a short time, the dark-haired woman emerges from the front door carrying my plastic laundry basket filled with sundry items.

"What did you say to them?" I ask, as she pushes the basket in the back of her truck.

"I told them I know what you need," she says climbing into the front seat.

As we drive, I listen to this woman, this stranger, tell me about herself and her family: how she and her two daughters from a prior marriage live with her along with her second husband. She tells me that she is helping to raise his young daughter, too. "You'll have the lower level all to yourself," she says. "There's a full bathroom down there and a meditation space." She tells me she will cook for me – three vegetarian meals a day – that she will teach me about eating clean and the importance of juicing and natural supplements. "Also, we have a pool so you can swim if you want," she says. "And we can do yoga on my back porch."

I can hardly wrap my brain around what I'm being offered. I look at the way she is gripping the steering wheel. She appears to be in complete control of her big truck, her own life, and now mine too.

"Why are you doing this?" I ask.

The dark-haired is careful and keeps her eyes on the road. "Because I've been through something like you're going through," she says. "And someone helped me get through it."

I figure we'd better get things cleared up straight away so that she can change her mind. "I don't have any money," I tell her. "I can't pay you." I wait for her to slam on the breaks, to pull over to the side of the road, and drop me off right then and there.

"I don't expect payment," she says. "I just know something good will come from our meeting like this."

I wonder if I've made a mistake, if I've landed with a person who is perhaps looking for a best friend or a domestic worker.

"I don't think you understand how sick I am," I say.

"There's nothing for you to do," she insists. "Except get well."

As we turn onto a long, quiet road, the countryside rolls by in a yellow blur. Sitting in the car, I realize I'm being offered something strange and precious: love and companionship, validation and understanding. I hardly know what to do with it.

"Since you're coming home with me and all, you should probably tell me your name," the woman says.

"Renée," I say.

The woman driving the car takes her eyes off the road for a moment and looks at me before erupting into laughter. "Your name is Renée?" she asks.

"Yes," I say. "Why are you laughing?"

"My name is Renee, too," she says. "What do you think about that?"

It's a strange moment, one that feels magical, even mystical.

In Jewish culture, the Yiddish word "bashert" is often translated to mean "soulmate"; however, the concept of bashert is much more than finding love by being at the right place at the right time. The literal meaning of the word is "destiny," and the implication is that God has had a hand in bringing you to that moment, thereby helping you to orchestrate your part in the destiny of the world.

For me, meeting Renee McLain is bashert.

CHAPTER 16

RE-EDUCATION

Located on several acres of land, Renee's house is a large bright contemporary colonial with a backyard orchard filled with ripe apple trees. Inside, her eldest daughter, Madison, a high school senior, is doing her math homework while seated on a stool at a granite-topped kitchen island. When Renee introduces me, announcing that I'll be staying in the guest bedroom for an indefinite period of time, I'm surprised by Madison's lack of response.

"I hope it isn't too weird for you, having a stranger in the house," I say.

Madison shrugs. "You're not the first stray mom has brought to stay with us," she says, rattling off the names of other people who have come and gone. Madison explains that each of the other people have also come through difficult life situations, many of which have been complicated by prescription drugs.

After a time, Renee takes me downstairs to a dimly lit space furnished with a queen-sized bed and two night tables, an oversized desk, a chest of drawers, and an upright piano. Just outside the bedroom, there is a common area with a large television and a wood burning stove, and at the far end of the common area, there is a bathroom with a shower exclusively for my use. I unpack what few items I have and lie down on the bed.

It feels magical to have landed in such a fortuitous situation. I think about how, just a few hours earlier, I was considering taking my own life. And somehow here I am, being welcomed into the home of a loving, nurturing family with a woman who reassures me that she has gone through a similar situation and healed. I can hardly believe my good fortune.

Several hours later, Renee calls me upstairs for dinner where I meet the rest of the McLain Family: Renee's younger daughter, Emily; Renee's husband, Harry; and his elementary school-aged daughter, Audrey. Despite the fact that I am in the middle of a psychotic episode and feeling dissociated and debilitated, I try to act as normally as possible, and while everyone else enjoys their chicken and salad, I introduce myself and attempt to explain the ordeal I've been going through.

"Don't you know drugs are bad for you?" eight-year old Audrey asks.

Though she is only in 3rd grade, I find myself feeling strangely defensive. "I wasn't using street drugs," I tell her. "I was taking prescription medication from a doctor."

Audrey shrugs, clearly underwhelmed by my answer. "Drugs are drugs," she says, taking a bite of chicken.

When the meal is over, the children retire to their bedrooms to complete their homework, and I attempt to make myself useful by clearing the dishes from the dining room table. The entire time, my head feels like a helium-filled balloon attached to a long string. The world is pulsing and pixelated, and I am unsteady on my feet. The walk from the dining room to the kitchen is physically exhausting, and I end up unintentionally dropping a drinking glass, which shatters on the hardwood floor.

While Renee picks up the largest pieces, Harry disappears to get a broom and dustpan. My heart is palpitating, and I'm more nauseous than I've ever been. For weeks now, I've been moving into and out of a dissociative state, where I don't feel attached to my physical body. I know I must look crazy, but I can't pull myself together. Filled with an overwhelming sense of panic, I drop to my hands and knees. I can feel myself coming undone right then and there in that beautiful kitchen, in that beautiful house.

"I'll do better," I say, sobbing. "I promise I won't make any more messes."

Renee and Harry exchange glances, and I'm certain they are going to put me out on the street for my infraction. "It's just a glass," Harry says. "Don't worry about it."

"We drop things around here all the time," Renee says.

I stare at my hosts, feeling like an alien. In my family, messes are not well tolerated. Spilled milk is a serious offense. There is a right way to do things and a wrong way to do them, and a broken drinking glass would be used as clear evidence of doing something the wrong way. It would have been an opportunity to shame and blame. As it was in my parents' home, so it was in the house I shared with my husband. I was reminded time and again that I was fed, clothed, and had a roof over my head – and that my need for occasional emotional reassurance was over the top.

I think about the many times over the course of my life that I've received the message that I'm a "bad girl" for not simply going along with the way others expect me to behave.

In the McLain house, I begin to see that perhaps being a nice, agreeable girl is not the best way to live. I realize I've been discouraged from talking about the many complicated traumas in my life. Renee encourages me to break the silence and share my feelings. She teaches me about the nature of my injury, how benzodiazepines have sedative, hypnotic (sleep-inducing), anxiolytic (anti-anxiety), anticonvulsant, and muscle relaxant properties. She tells me benzos have a slight amnesic effect and that, because of this, they interfere with the pain center, effectively masking traumas that people experience during the course of their lives. She informs me that part of the work I will have to do involves re-experiencing the traumas I've had during my life and instead of processing them cognitively, now I will be processing them somatically. "You're going to feel emotions more intensely than you've ever felt them before," Renee says.

For the first few weeks of October, Renee and I go outside to practice yoga and meditate together. Sometimes, she insists that I accompany her on errands, but most of the time, I hide in my little room in the basement.

• • •

Eventually, the seasons change. The leaves turn red, then brown and drop off the trees. What few clothes I have are no longer appropriate for autumn in Upstate New York. Around the end of October, Renee orders me a few pairs of pants from off the Internet and she gives me several sweatshirts to borrow; Harry lets me wear his wool socks.

During the months I stay at the McLains' house, I'm unable to handle anything that requires electricity. Whenever I touch the handle of a vacuum cleaner, a hair dryer, a blender or some other electric device, a surge of intensely uncomfortable energy courses through my body. In addition to these invisible, internal vibrations, I am suffering from both akathisia -- an inability to sit still -- and tardive dyskinesia -- involuntary, repetitive movements including twitching, tremoring, grimacing, and blinking. These uncomfortable movement disorders are often associated with neuroleptic drugs, and they are some of the main reasons why people choose to commit suicide during benzodiazepine withdrawal. [8]

During this time, I'm extremely self-conscious about the lack of control I have over my body. I don't look right. I don't feel right. I'm not me. Because I can't hold my phone or even touch the keypad, Renee occasionally speaks to my parents and my husband on my behalf and tells them to await further instructions regarding visitation. It's a time of great introspection for me, and I realize the reason they call it "withdrawal" is because you have to withdraw to do it.

While convalescing in the McLains' house, my parents put my name on a prayer list at their synagogue, and they ask the rabbi to pay me a visit. Rabbi Seymour has been officiating at Temple Adath Yeshurun for as long as my parents have been members there. When I was growing up, my cousins babysat his children, and he officiated my wedding. I'm used to seeing him in long, formal robes with a yarmulke on his head, but on the day he appears at Renee's house, he looks like a regular guy in his navy-blue sweatshirt, jeans, and sneakers.

The two of us sit on the couch in Renee's living room, exchanging pleasantries. "Your parents asked me to come," he says. "They're worried about you." Looking around, Rabbi Seymour acknowledges that I've landed in a good place.

Clearly, he can see I'm in a beautiful home, that I'm being well cared for. "So, what's going on?" he asks.

Less than three months into acute withdrawal, I'm completely out of my mind. The world inside the house and outside the window is perpetually shifting and gyrating. I try my best to explain to the rabbi what is happening to me without sounding like a crazed lunatic.

From the start, my experience in withdrawal has felt strangely Biblical in proportion, and it feels natural to speak to the rabbi in parables that I learned many decades earlier while in religious school.

"Remember when God commands Abraham to offer his son as a sacrifice?" I begin. "Abraham doesn't want to do it – being asked to kill his son is a devastating request -- but his faith is so strong that he's willing to do whatever God asks --. . ."

"Sure," Rabbi Seymour says. He looks at me without judgment, and I feel comfortable enough to continue.

"And God doesn't only test Abraham. He tests Noah, too, by commanding him to build an ark in his backyard. Remember that?" I ask.

Rabbi Seymour nods.

"All Noah's neighbors laugh at him when they see him building that ark. He tries to tell them a flood is coming, but they won't listen to him. 'There's not a cloud in the sky,' they say. But Noah's faith is strong, so he does what God asks him to do. And he and his family survive a flood that destroys the world . . ." I pause to look out the window, at the apple trees ripe with fruit, before turning back to the rabbi who sits motionless beside me. "I feel like I'm being commanded to do something, too," I say.

Despite the fact that I am doing and saying some strange – even alarming -- things, Rabbi Seymour remains calm. He listens intently and looks me in the eye. "What can I do to help you?" he asks.

Up until this point, no one has asked me this question. Nearly everyone has assumed they know what is best for me; they give me what they assume they might want or need if they were in my shoes.

"I don't think you can do anything," I say. "Basically, I'm awaiting my next instruction."

Rabbi Seymour's face changes into something that feels like a smile. "You're going to be okay, kiddo," he says, patting me on the hand.

"How can you say that?" I ask. "How do you know?"

Rabbi Seymour shares with me a little bit about his own life, some of which I know, but much of which I don't. He tells me about how – many years before -- his son suffered a catastrophic stroke following a high-risk brain surgery; how his four-year-old son's mind was intact but that he would never walk or talk, feed himself, or breathe independently again. Rabbi Seymour tells me his feelings surrounding this tragedy and shares his feelings about God. "At the time, I thought to myself: 'Why me?' and 'How can I ever survive this?' But you know what? You can and you do." He tells me about his wife – the new role she took on as their son's primary caregiver, about his other children, how everyone's love grew and brought healing into the wounded places. "You're on a journey," Rabbi Seymour says. "It's going to be unpleasant for a while, but you'll get to the other side."

A short while later, the two of us walk outside. As the fall leaves skitter across the driveway, I feel the autumn breeze pressing against my skin. "One thing is ending and another thing is beginning," the rabbi says before getting into his car.

Outside of this one brief visit from Rabbi Seymour, my husband and son are my only other visitors. They come once, right after Thanksgiving. It's a strained visit during which time the three of us sit stiffly, side-by-side on the McLain's living room couch. I ask Cal a lot of questions about school, which he answers politely. Neither my husband nor my son ask me how I am feeling, and they stay for less than two hours. I feel extremely guilty about not being able to take care of my son during this time, and I worry that his needs are not being met.

"Cal hasn't missed a single beat," Derek says confidently, draping one arm around our son's neck. "He's been getting high grades in school and he's still fencing, so really, not that much has changed."

Derek's insistence that my extended absence from our home has not negatively impacted our son hurts my feelings, and Cal seems to sense my upset.

"Just get better, Mom," he says. "Get better so that you can come home."

After waving goodbye to my husband and son, I stand outside and watch Derek's car disappear down the road followed by a cloud of dust. Feeling isolated, unloved, and forgotten, I retreat to the basement.

• • •

While living in the McLains' house, Renee introduces me to Somato Respiratory Integration (SRI) and the power of breath-work. Developed in the 1980s by world-renowned practitioner, Donald Epstein, SRI teaches the brain and body how to connect and release stored tension, which may appear as illness or disease. SRI enables the body's own self-generated mechanisms of movement and respiration to assist in the transformation of stress, tension, and interference to the nervous system. A certified practitioner of Epstein's SRI techniques, Renee teaches me about the relationship between breath and grief. Several times each day, Renee tells me to lie flat on my back with one hand on my chest and one hand on my belly. I tuck in my chin and focus on a set of patterned breathing techniques, feeling my ribs expand and contract, my chest and belly rising and falling.

One afternoon, Renee says we will be going deeper into our SRI practice. She tells me to bend my knees, tuck my chin, and breathe in the way she has instructed me to in the past, but this time, the pace she sets for me is faster. After a short while, I'm breathing so quickly, I actually feel like I've been running in a race.

"Upper . . . Middle . . . Lower . . ." Renee prompts, as I breathe in through my nose and out through my mouth. "Faster," she says.

SRI breath-work is more strenuous than people might appreciate. It requires a great deal of concentration on the part of the practitioner as well as the participant. After a while, I feel as if a motor has started up inside my chest.

"Put your hands over your head," Renee says.

I hear Renee's directions, but my arms feel too heavy to lift. I'm tired and I feel like I could easily fall into a deep sleep, but Renee isn't finished yet. After separating my hands that have been resting one over the other atop my chest, she pulls each hand so that they are on either side of my head. My elbows are bent and my palms are facing up.

Suddenly, there is a bright light behind my eyes, and when it recedes, I can see myself.

• • •

I'm on a bed surrounded by beige sheets. My body is full and soft curls frame my face. A man has covered both of my legs with one of his own so I can't wiggle out from underneath him. He doesn't get off of me even when I ask. A pinecone falls from a tree onto the slate roof above us, and I startle. I tell him to stop but his mouth is hard and sloppy on mine. He is kissing me, but he isn't kissing me. I could be anyone. He jams something stiff inside me, and then lowers his head beside my right ear. When I turn to look at him, I see his eyes are shut. Feeling every thrust, every stab, it is like he is punching holes inside of me. Be quiet, he says. Big girls don't cry.

• • •

I hear myself screaming, a sound that goes on for many minutes. My body buzzes and my hands and feet move in tiny circles, along with my hips. Energetically, I'm in an odd space: simultaneously reliving a memory as if it is happening, but also completely aware that what I'm experiencing is not real. After a while, I stop screaming. My body stops moving, and I open my eyes.

“You’ve been holding your breath and keeping your pain hidden behind a locked door for a long time,” Renee says, smoothing my hair. “Breath work is a way of accessing that door.”

After confiding in Renee about the rape that occurred many decades prior, she explains that people sometimes push uncomfortable body memories aside in an effort to avoid feeling them fully. “You’ve created a shadow-self,” Renee says, and she explains that to heal, it will be necessary to change my perceptions about all that I have previously judged or labeled as bad. “You’re learning how to coexist with all the unpleasant parts of your reality, rather than seeing them as things to hide or repress,” Renee says. “When people forgive themselves and love themselves, when they are honest about who they are – when they can speak candidly about the difficulties they’ve been through, when they can articulate honestly what they want and need, that is when people heal,” she says.

Over the next weeks, Renee takes me to an acupuncturist and brings a massage therapist to me. I meet with a nutritionist who informs me that my body is depleted of many important nutrients necessary for maintaining optimum health. I am introduced to magnesium glycinate (which I take in high doses every evening), and I begin other supplements, too. Up until this point, I’ve never paid much attention to my diet; I’ve always been a healthy eater – but the nutritionist explains how fruits and vegetables grown decades ago were much richer in vitamins and minerals than the varieties most of us get today.

Renee pays for all of these services, and she never asks me for a single penny.

While staying at her house, I come across a book by Robert Whitaker – *Anatomy of an Epidemic*: *Magic Bullets, Psychiatric Drugs, and the Astonishing Rise of Mental Illness in America* – which argues that psychotropic drugs are causing as much — if not more — harm than good and that the drugs hailed as the cure for mental disorders instead worsen them over the long term.[9]

Whitaker's book shines a light on a feeling that I've always had but have never been able to articulate: that the drugs I've been turning to for help have actually been harming me. For over a decade, I've been told that there is something wrong with me -- that I am too much -- and suddenly all of my assumptions are being challenged. Maybe there was nothing wrong with me at all. Maybe my body was simply responding naturally to trauma. Maybe my limbic system switched on and never switched off. Maybe I didn't know how to ask for what I needed. Or maybe I asked and others simply did not know how to meet my needs.

•••

One gray afternoon, Harry comes home with a Christmas tree and everyone gathers to hang ornaments. It's strange to be without my family, celebrating a holiday I did not grow up observing, and even though Renee gives me a stocking filled with little gifts, I feel like an intruder.

On New Year's Eve, while the rest of the McLain family is out celebrating, I watch the clock flip from 11:59 PM to midnight. It is 2014 now, and I have been disabled for four months. After lying on my bed for a long time, I finally fall into a kind of restless sleep, and a few hours later, I hear someone feeding the wood fire right outside my bedroom door. It is Harry, and, after he goes upstairs, I try to go back to sleep but find I am wide-awake.

For many months now, I've been getting only a few hours of rest each night. Without enough sleep, the brain and the body do not function properly. Sleep deprivation affects every major system in the body and can cause cognition problems, immune system disorders, respiratory issues, hormonal imbalance, delusions, and hallucinations. Many people complain about experiencing a relentless ringing in their ears (tinnitus) that intensifies when they lie down, and nearly everyone experiences night terrors.

Hours pass and I still cannot sleep. Feeling cold and lonely, I wrap myself in my blanket and go out to lie down on the floor next to the wood-burning stove. Many times, during withdrawal, I have the experience that I am moving when I am, in fact, still. Suddenly, I have a feeling that I'm being pulled toward the fire, feet first. Despite the fact that the door to the wood stove is closed, I feel my body passing through the glass window. Clutching the carpet, I strain to prevent myself from being devoured by the flames. A moment later, I can see and smell my flesh burning; I believe I am being incinerated alive.

It is a nightmare not unlike the one I had during the Near-Death Experience after my son was born in 1999. Feeling my body moving against my will is a sensory experience so real that I am certain I am crossing over the fine line between sanity and insanity once and for all.

Shaking with terror, I scream for help at the top of my lungs.

Immediately, I hear footsteps coming downstairs. A light flickers on, and Renee appears wearing a white nightshirt. She looks tired, and I instantly feel terrible for waking her. She doesn't say a word, not even to ask me what's wrong. Instead, she lies down on the floor beside me and curls her body around mine. She holds me in her arms and rocks me like a baby.

“I can’t do this!” I say. “I need someone to save me!”

Renee reminds me to breathe, so I do. “Sweet girl,” she whispers in my ear. “Don’t you see? You’re going to have to save yourself.”

CHAPTER 17
ANGEL

Renee stays with me on the floor for most of that night, and in the wee morning hours, just as the sun is coming up, she adds more wood to the fire and tiptoes upstairs. Back in the guest bedroom, I slide under the covers and try to rest.

During this time, I notice that I can sometimes feel myself hovering at an in-between place, neither fully awake nor fully asleep. I am as relaxed as possible while still maintaining some sense of consciousness. It is in this strange place and space that I begin to hear a low hum.

Ancient teachings and modern science agree that all things in existence are made up at their most essential level of vibrating, pulsing energy. For millennia, mystics have recounted their experience of this energy, which is said to manifest itself in our hearing awareness as a humming vibration around and within everything else.

But in this moment, I don't know any of this.

All I know is that I am listening to something that sounds like a combination of a gentle, pulsing motor and prayer, if you were listening to these things from a great distance away. With my eyes closed, I see psychedelic splotches of color – purple and yellow and pink – out of which a robed figure emerges. Taller and more beautiful than most human beings, the figure is essentially genderless, but seems more feminine than masculine to me. She has a single set of wings and her face is turned upward, as if she is waiting for someone else to appear.

"Listen to The Voice," she says. *"If you listen to The Voice, you will never be led astray."*

I want to say something, but my tongue is thick in my mouth and my eyes feel heavy and weighted.

• • •

Somehow, I am in the Adirondack Mountains, surrounded by trees and gigantic rocks. It is August of 1982, and I'm with my friends from summer camp. It is dark outside and, while everyone is outside listening to ghost stories by the fire, I am alone in my tent.

I remember this day as if it were yesterday. It is the day I sliced my toe open on something sharp, and I had to be driven to a local Boy Scout Camp to receive several stitches – without anesthesia. I've been given crutches to use, but they are hard to manage on the uneven ground. I worry about being a burden to my friends, about being unable to keep up with everyone on the trails, about being left behind. Listening to my friends laughing and clapping in unison, I feel lonely, and it is a great relief when my tent-mates finally finish eating marshmallows and come in to settle for the night.

It's cold outside. My breath hovers in the mountain air, and I adjust myself inside my sleeping bag in an attempt to stay warm. Eventually, the sound of rustling leaves lulls me to sleep.

At some point, I awake with a throbbing toe. Despite my discomfort, I keep my eyes closed and remain silent so as not to wake my friends.

That's when I hear someone whisper my name.

Opening my eyes, I'm surprised to see my grandmother Muriel, my mother's mother, sitting beside me. She's wearing a white nightgown and matching slippers, the fuzzy slides she prefers. "I'm sorry to wake you," she says.

My grandmother and I are very close. The two of us have been known to sit for hours, playing cards or doing puzzles. She takes me horseback riding and we work together in her magnificent garden.

I'm stunned. *How in the world did she find me in the middle of the woods? And where is Grandpa?*

"I have to go," she whispers.

Where? I think. *Where do you have to go?*

"Know that you are loved…" she says, "… and that I'll be watching over you."

I close my eyes for a second, just long enough to blink, and when I open them again, I see a sliver of my grandmother's white nightgown swish through the tent in a place where there is no door. Filled with a sense of deep knowing, I shimmy out of my sleeping bag and open the tent flap. Crawling outside on my hands and knees, I look up at the sky.

I can feel it in my bones.

My grandmother has died.

The next morning at breakfast, I tell everyone about what happened to me.

"It's impossible," one counselor asserts, rolling his eyes. "That was just a dream." One person after another provides me with all kinds of logical excuses for what I have experienced. People make fun of me and call me a liar. My friends don't want to hear about voices and visions, about intuition and things that cannot be explained or measured. *The pain made you hallucinate*, they insist, and while I try to hold on to the specialness of it all, after a while, I, too, start to doubt what happened.

• • •

Two weeks later, I return from summer camp, exhausted and eager to eat homemade food, shower without flip-flops, and sleep in my own bed. As I walk down the bus steps, dusty, rumpled and in need of a haircut, I see my father standing alone. He tosses my duffel bag over his shoulder, and I drag my trunk across the parking lot. Once everything is loaded into the car, we get inside. My father hesitates and stares straight ahead. His hands grip the steering wheel, and he takes a breath.

"I know what you're going to say," I tell him. "Grandma died, right?"

My father looks at me, bewildered.

I tell him about my experience that night in the Adirondacks. How every night since, I've had visions of my grandmother, lying on her back in her garden with a Japanese beetle pinched between her thumb and forefinger.

My father tells me there has been a funeral; that all my relatives and my grandmother's friends came to mourn together, that the synagogue had been packed. He tells me my mother is busy fulfilling her responsibilities as the executor of the estate by mailing out the items bequeathed in my grandmother's will. "We went through all the emotions," my father says. "Now there are a lot of practical things we need to do."

On the way to Liberty, New York, I weep like a baby. My grandmother was my closest friend and confidante. I can't imagine life without long, relaxed vacations in her little white house with the red shutters. Having been away at summer camp for eight weeks, I've stockpiled stories that I'd wanted to share with her. I can already feel myself missing our regular Sunday night telephone calls.

Four hours later, my father and I arrive at a tiny cemetery in the Catskill Mountains, and he directs me to a patch of lumpy soil. I can't believe my grandmother is inside a box buried underground. My father stands nearby as I try to wrap my head around this terrible new reality. It feels strange to cry alone, and I ache for my camp friends to put their arms around me and help me to mourn this loss.

For the rest of the summer, I walk around feeling lonely and disconnected from my family.

The following month, when school starts up again, I visit the school nurse. After she checks my height and my weight, I tell her about my prophetic dream the night my grandmother died and how sad I am that she is gone.

"It's best to keep things like that to yourself," the nurse says. She makes a gesture indicating I should zip my lips, secure my mouth with a tiny lock, and throw away the key.

It is terrible advice repeated too many times over the course of my life, and I take it to heart.

• • •

Coming out of my flashback, I'm strangely aware that I've been time-traveling in a kind of altered state of awareness. Moving from events that happened in the distant past, I return to my bedroom in Renee's basement to find the angel-like figure still hovering in front of me.

"Listen to The Voice," the figure says again, before shooting straight upward, until she is no larger than a single star in the night sky. Immediately, I feel myself surrounded by the love of my ancestors. Both of my grandmothers are there; my grandfathers, too. I feel many hands touching me, energy being exchanged. I know I am with family, with people who genuinely love me, and I feel a sense of deep knowing.

"You are going to Heal," the Voice says. "It will not be easy, so you must have Faith."

• • •

I think about the words Renee has said, about how I am going to have to save myself, and I feel something shift inside of me. Though her words were not particularly reassuring, I understand what she means. Life has presented me with a situation that I don't know how to handle, and the simplest things seem like insurmountable obstacles. In the past, I would have put my issues in the hands of others, transferred blame, relied on someone or something else – a parent, a husband, a doctor, a friend, a pill. But in this moment, I realize I cannot depend on others to save me, show me the way, or give me the answers.

No one person can save another.

All of us must save ourselves and find the best methods to do so.

That piece of truth is the toughest pill I have ever had to swallow.

CHAPTER 18
OUT OF REACH

On New Year's Day, I open a fresh journal filled with college-lined paper, and the first thing I do is scribble '2014' inside the front cover of the jacket. Just six months prior, I'd been a regular blogger and, while staying at Renee's, it occurs to me that my readers might be wondering why I've disappeared. While writing is normally my strongpoint, something I have always been able to do rather effortlessly, it takes me forever to compose even a few sentences. Though I hardly know how to articulate what has been happening to me, I have a strong sense of obligation to inform people about what I do know – and that is that abruptly stopping benzodiazepines is a very bad idea. I promise myself that if I ever get to the other side of this injury that I'll do my best to share what I've learned so that no one else is injured in the way I've been injured.

A few hours before dinner, Renee comes downstairs to sit beside me on the bed. She tells me that she and her family will be going out of town on vacation in February, and she wonders what I would like to do. "Do you want to go home to Rochester while we are away?" she asks.

At this point, I haven't seen my husband or my son in many months, and I'm nervous about what it will feel like to return to my family after being away for so long.

That night, I call Derek to tell him that I'd like to return to Rochester, and he is amenable to the idea. A week or two later, Renee and I pull into the driveway outside my home.

It's late afternoon: Cal is still at fencing practice, and Derek is still at work. No one is there to meet me or welcome me, and – at the time – I don't think much about this. Over the years, I've gotten used to being alone a lot. Though Derek and I have been a couple for nearly two decades, I've been trained to handle most things by myself.

Using my key, I open the front door and Renee follows me in. Being back is strange. For the most part, everything looks exactly the way I've left it. The family room is spotless, but the curtains are drawn – something I never do – so the room is dark. When I open the blinds, the cat wakes and looks at me from his place on the ottoman, but even he doesn't move to greet me. I give Renee a quick tour and acclimate myself at the same time: the decorative pillows on the sofa have been removed, there are cobwebs on the chandelier, and an unattractive oversized chair has been relocated to the office.

In the master bedroom, I experience the kind of sensation a person might have if that person were standing too close to a power line.

"Do you feel that?" I ask Renee.

"You're awake now," she says. "You're going to feel a lot of things."

• • •

After Renee leaves, I sit on the couch with the cat. We look at each other, and I apologize to him for disappearing so abruptly. He narrows his eyes, then hops off the couch and settles himself on the rug a short distance away. A little while later, the garage door goes up, and I realize I'm not quite sure what to do.

Should I go outside to greet my husband and son? Or do I wait for them to come inside?

After a few moments, they are in the mudroom, taking off their boots and coats.

"Hi Mom," my son says casually, dropping his backpack on the floor, as if I hadn't been gone for a minute. He comes over to me and hooks his arm around my neck in much the way he might hug one of his pals from summer camp. Cal asks me a few questions about my trip, about how I am feeling, and then turns to his father. "I'm hungry," he says. "What are we making for dinner?"

From across the room, my husband smiles at me weakly, as if I'm broken. While I wasn't exactly sure how we would greet each other after being apart for so long, I definitely expected that there would be some glimmer of warmth. But instead of coming toward me, Derek walks into the kitchen, opens the refrigerator, and sticks his head inside. As my husband and son discuss the merits of chicken over fish, I become overwhelmed with emotion. Making meals has always been my job, and while I should be grateful that they have figured out how to take care of themselves in my absence, I feel like a stranger in a strange land. They have a new rhythm and I am not part of their new groove. This is the longest I've ever been away from my family, and I feel completely superfluous.

In my absence, Derek has reclaimed the master bedroom, and because I am still suffering from chemically induced insomnia, I offer to move into the guest bedroom. For the next month, my husband and son resume their normal routines, which don't include me. They exit the house early each morning, leaving me alone for between 8-10 hours a day.

During this time, my physical and mental symptoms are so intense that I cry all day long, repeatedly reminding myself to be patient, but it is very hard. I set two goals for myself each day, one of which is taking a shower, and on some days, it feels nearly impossible to meet that goal. The other thing I commit to doing is taking a daily walk, and each day, no matter the weather, I wander the trails in my suburban neighborhood.

February in Rochester, New York is a gloomy month, and this day, the thermometer registers below thirty degrees. As I put on my long, black puffer coat, a hat, scarf, and gloves, I hear the weatherman warning people about black ice. "It's slippery out there," he says.

Outside, the air is cold and dry, and it takes my breath away. There is a particular tree I always pass, an enormous maple that towers over three stories high. For years, I have watched this tree sprout and shed its leaves, and on this morning, tiny icicles cling to every branch. I think about the tree, how heavy and weighed down it looks. I feel the season reflecting my emotions, and I wonder if I will ever know the joy of springtime again. The pavement beneath my feet is slick, and my trendy snow boots – though warm – don't provide much traction.

After trudging around for a while, I approach another part of the neighborhood trail. Flanked by tall brown grasses, the muddy pond is usually obscured from sight, but heavy ice has caused two trees to fall, opening up a clear view to the water, which has clearly frozen-over. At that precise moment, the sun appears from behind the clouds, causing the ice to sparkle brightly. Something about the view draws me to it, and I leave the trail and move toward the water's edge. Testing the ice carefully, I make sure that it will support my weight, and when it does, I take tentative steps, moving further toward the center of the pond. When I reach the middle of the frozen pond, the wind blows bitter cold, and the sun retreats behind the clouds again.

That's when I hear it: a weird high-pitched ricochet followed by a squeak and a groan.

An instant later, my feet fall out from underneath me.

I'm underwater.

Water rushes into my nose and mouth, and when I try to come up for air, my hands bump up against the ice overhead. When I finally find the opening and come to the surface, coughing and sputtering, I gasp for breath. My hair covers my eyes, and as I strain to get some sense of my bearings, I can feel my boots, heavy on my feet. After trying to hoist myself out of the icy pond several times, to no avail, I begin to panic. My waterlogged coat is pulling me down. *You haven't come this far to die in this goddamned pond,* I think to myself.

Grabbing onto some flattened cattails, I somehow manage to extricate myself from the rotten ice, wade through the chilly marsh, and climb back onto the trail.

Soaking wet and covered in mud, I decide to walk back home on the road, not far from the pond. I'm sobbing hysterically as I trudge up the normally busy street, which, for some reason, on this day is light on traffic.

When I am nearly home, a gray mini-van approaches. I recognize it as belonging to someone I know well and have always considered a friend. Our sons have attended religious school together since they were toddlers, and our families have shared many dinners and holidays together. I feel a sense of relief, knowing with absolute certainty, this friend will pull over to assist me. In anticipation of the warmth of her car, I stop walking and raise my hand to wave.

It is a complete shock to me when the mini-van blows past.

Prior to my brain injury, I frequently socialized with people from work, the neighborhood, and synagogue. I loved going to coffee shops and out for meals. But in this moment, standing in the street, I feel completely invisible. I realize I haven't seen or talked to this friend or anyone else in nearly half a year. I have fallen completely off everyone's radar. I recognize that my friends are busy with their own lives, and I feel I no longer belong anywhere.

Many people going through post-acute benzodiazepine withdrawal experience a complete deterioration of their social lives following the injury. There are numerous reasons why isolation occurs. Outside of the hundreds of bizarre physical and mental symptoms people in protracted withdrawal are forced to endure, noisy environments and fatigue make socializing a challenge. Additionally, folks in withdrawal often feel the people in their lives simply cannot understand the effects of our condition. The strange, sometimes mystical experiences we have -- paired with our lost sense of self-care are difficult for family and friends to accept, and many people slowly drop away over time.

• • •

A few days before Valentine's Day of 2014, I wake up in the guest bedroom, alone. I'm aware that I have been getting sicker since I've returned to Rochester to be with my family. Being alone all day, isolated during the cold winter months while suffering from the symptoms associated with benzodiazepine withdrawal takes its toll on me.

One morning, my son comes in to say goodbye like he does every morning before heading off to school. On this day, I'm in a particularly bad wave and my symptoms are flaring. My body is buzzing and I can hear bubbling and popping sounds inside my head.

"Will you do something for me?" I ask.

My son answers hesitantly. "Maybe," he offers, cautiously as if he's being asked a trick question.

"See that pillow?" I ask, pointing to a cushion just out of my reach. "Will you hold it over my head until I stop breathing," I say. "Will you do that for me?"

Cal takes two steps away from my bed. "No," he says. "I'm not doing that."

"Please!" I sob. "I can't read or write. I can't drive. I'm in pain. I can't participate in life, and I may be like this forever. I can't do this anymore."

My son looks at me with fear in his eyes as I continue to beg him to help free me of the pain that I've been enduring without a break for nearly six months.

"I'd rather have you here on the planet, in this bed, not able to do anything than not have you here," Cal says. His voice cracks, and I see tears streaming down his cheeks as he walks out of the bedroom, closing the door behind him.

A few minutes later, Derek appears at my bedside. He's understandably upset that I've made such a terrible request of our son, and a few hours later I find myself sitting in my psychiatrist's office where my husband and my doctor discuss places I might be able to go for rehabilitation.

The prospect of being surrounded by a community of people who are going through similar experiences sounds good to me. Dr. Halligan flips through brochures and she and Derek discuss the pros and cons of each program. "There's a place in California," she says. "And there's a place in Phoenix that's supposed to be good."

Both options sound too far away, but I'm tired of being alone.

Of fighting alone.

"I think you're going to thrive in the program I'm recommending," Dr. Halligan says. "My guess is that you're going to feel much better within the next six months."

I have no choice but to believe her.

CHAPTER 19
ARIZONA

The flight to Arizona is excruciating, and when I look back at it now, I truly do not know how I managed to do it. Unwilling to take time off from work, my husband puts his mother in his place, and she helps me pack a small bag of clothing and toiletries and accompanies me to Arizona. I've always had a good relationship with my mother-in-law, and during the trip she holds my hand and keeps the conversation light.

To everyone else on the plane, the flight is calm, but to me, the ride feels wildly turbulent. Any adaptive mechanism I have ever drawn on during times of difficulty is simply not available. Benzodiazepine withdrawal is like being stuck in a hurricane, where all the windows are being blown out continuously, non-stop. There is no respite. Outside my little oval window, I watch a kaleidoscope of nitrogen and oxygen particles swirl around the silver body of the airplane.

"Do you see that?" I ask my mother-in-law.

She is worried about me and suggests I close the window shade if the light is bothersome.

When we land, my mother-in-law escorts me to the area where I'm supposed to meet a driver who will transport me to my final destination, about forty-five minutes away.

"I'm going to visit an old friend from college," she says before giving me a hug goodbye.

After a full day of travel, I arrive at The Meadows of Wickenburg just after midnight on Valentine's Day. The nation's premier treatment program for trauma, addiction, codependency, depression, and eating disorders, the Meadows' campus is nestled in the Sonoran Desert, making it an ideal location to focus on recovery.

The intake process is emotionally exhausting. I am asked hundreds of questions meant to assess my mental acuity. When we finish, a woman rifles through my belongings and takes away my plastic razor and nail clippers. A nurse assigns me to a room in the women's quarters, and I follow her through a series of dark corridors until we reach the room where I will reside for my first three days, while I am monitored by the staff.

When the nurse opens the door, I catch the first glimpse of my roommate who is sleeping in a single bed pressed up against the wall. I'm assigned a shelf and a closet. The nurse points to another door and tells there is a toilet, sink and shower stall on the other side. As I unzip my suitcase to find a nightshirt, she asks if I need anything else and informs me that someone will be at the nurses' station all night, should I need help.

I spend most of that first night crying. My life feels like a crazy movie, and I can't figure out how I've wound up at an in-patient psychiatric hospital. It doesn't make sense: I went to school, got good grades, went to college, graduated with honors, got a job, married, and had a child. Didn't I do everything I was supposed to do and in the right order?

The next morning, I meet my roommate and the two of us head toward the dining room for breakfast. On the way, a fight breaks out between two female residents who lunge at each other, screaming. Two male attendants dressed in white uniforms show up to pull the women off each other. I learn that these kinds of outbursts are typical in rehabilitation settings since people coming off drugs can sometimes be combative.

It is important to mention that detox centers and other types of "rehab" situations are not appropriate settings for people withdrawing from prescription benzodiazepines. Accelerated detox is generally not considered the best way to treat patients who seek to discontinue benzodiazepines, as it is possible for people to experience life-threatening seizures (and even die) when medication cessation occurs in too rapid of a manner. I know many people who have been re-traumatized by their experiences in these kinds of facilities.

Fortunately, this is not my experience.

During my first few days at The Meadows, I'm sent for a battery of psychological and physiological tests, as well as blood-work and imaging, and outside of the fact that I have high levels of cortisol and low levels of Vitamin D, the scans reveal nothing of note. This stuns me because I am so clearly impaired. I meet with a psychiatrist and am assigned to a counselor on the Yellow Team, a group of five or six other residents who are also dealing with relational issues.

Getting a good night sleep at The Meadows is a real challenge. All night long, people come and go; the phone rings noisily at the nurses' station, and – on top of everything else – my roommate snores. I become a regular at the nurses' desk where I am given a pair of spongy, blue earplugs to try, but they don't help at all. Though I don't want to take any more drugs, I make an appointment with the psychiatrist who prescribes a combination of Buspar, Trazadone and Seroquel to help me rest. Around 9PM, everyone stands in line to receive their medication, dispensed in tiny paper cups. While the drugs may help some people to obtain restorative sleep, they simply snow me so that I cannot move my body to get out of bed. I take these pills exactly as prescribed during my entire stay at The Meadows, hoping I'm not causing further damage to my already kindled brain.

During the day, residential inpatient treatment centers offer a host of structured activities and therapies, and for the next two weeks, I follow a predictable routine. At The Meadows, early morning yoga is followed by a simple breakfast of granola and fruit. Afterwards, everyone attends a large group session led by soon-to-be "graduating" residents. During these meetings, we learn about the top news, weather, and sports headlines happening "on the outside." Morning meetings end with positive affirmations and the serenity prayer.

In a weird way, rehab at The Meadows feels a bit like college. Residents rotate from classroom to classroom in different buildings, but instead of meeting with professors and librarians, we meet with therapists and psychiatrists. During these sessions, counselors focus on topics related to the treatment process, and a significant focus during treatment is on achieving clarity about the issues, people and surroundings that fuel the desire to abuse drugs or alcohol.

I'm baffled.

"But I didn't abuse my medication," I tell my counselor. "I took is exactly as prescribed."

"In the beginning, taking benzodiazepines probably seemed like a harmless escape from whatever was going on in your life," he says. "But with prolonged use, the brain's chemistry begins to change. Instead of something you have control of, your brain begins signaling an intense need for the drug. What was once recreational becomes a habit that controls your life.

In full-blown addiction, the high isn't even the goal; it's often just using in order to feel somewhat normal." The counselor talks about how important it is to identify our own unique triggers so we can avoid relapsing post-treatment. "The first thirty days are the hardest," he says. "That's when most people relapse."

"What you're saying doesn't make sense," I say. "I haven't had any clonazepam in six months. When am I going to feel better?" I ask.

"Everyone is different," he says. "Whether it's prescription drugs obtained for legitimate medical reasons or illegal substances used recreationally, these substances take a physical and psychological toll that can't be underestimated."

While I am at The Meadows, my counselor tells me it is estimated that 25 percent of benzodiazepine users experience what's known as protracted withdrawal, a complicated phenomenon whereby a patient continues to experience a variety of intense sensory, motor, and neurological symptoms at the same level of intensity as if they did when the drug was first discontinued. "There is concern that long-term benzodiazepine use can cause irreversible functional changes in the central nervous system, as well as permanent structural damage," he says.

"Are you saying I might stay like this forever?" I ask.

"We really just don't know," my counselor says. "Currently, there aren't any studies to help us know the long-term effects of this kind of injury. And you know, many people in the protracted state commit suicide, so we never get a chance to really know what might have happened over time."

In a strange way, I really appreciate my time in rehab. Being with people are also going through intensely difficult times helps me to feel less alone. I develop a sense of fellowship with my Yellow Group members during the weeks in rehab, and as trust grows, we develop sincere compassion and understanding for each other's battles. A few of us form a little clique, sitting next to each other during meals and waving to each other during the course of the day. I haven't been outside of my social bubble in a very long time, and I'm intrigued by the fact that everyone is so different. Peter is a Latter-Day Saint with nine children; Marni is a Southern Belle who heads up a large not-for-profit agency; Todd is a physician from the Northeast; Judy lives in Nevada and is into fashion and makeup; Bradley is a soldier who has recently returned from his third tour in Afghanistan. Though we are all very different, our stories are remarkably similar: complicated trauma, paired with shame and a lack of self-care, a weak support system and an over-reliance on drugs and/or alcohol in an attempt to numb our feelings.

At the Meadows, patients participate in a host of therapeutic sessions, including individual and group therapy. There is a swimming pool, a high-ropes course, and a volleyball pit. In the evenings, we attend 12-Step meetings, play Ping-Pong, and have sing-alongs. We sit outside to talk and watch the sunset, or we gather around the one television watching "non-triggering" upbeat movies. The whole experience would have been fun, except for the fact that we are all completely cognitively scrambled, and the security guard who prowls around reminds us that we are not at summer camp.

While some prescription benzodiazepine users resent the 12-Step Approach to recovery, and feel the tenets of Alcoholics Anonymous do not really apply to their situations, I actually enjoy attending 12-Step meetings, which provide an opportunity for me to learn more about the other residents in the Meadows program. And while I'm not craving a drug or struggling to stay sober, I begin to realize that many people who end up medicating themselves identify with having less-than-nurturing, abusive family systems during childhood, which can lead to codependency patterns, addictions, mood disorders, even physical illness.

I'm surprised to learn that members of the clergy, distinguished military veterans, and well-known celebrities can also suffer from invisible ailments like low self-esteem, feelings of loss, disconnection, hopelessness, guilt and shame. The Meadows' counselors focus on underlying problems – including unresolved trauma -- and make it a goal to treat those things rather than focusing on a psychiatric diagnoses like "anxiety," "depression" or "substance use disorder." Each of us receives various physical, emotional, intellectual, creative and spiritual therapies to help us discover our strengths and remember who we truly are.

One night, during one of the requisite 12-Step meetings, an outside speaker comes to share his story about overcoming his addiction to alcohol. He talks about how, in his younger days, he'd lied, cheated, and stole money to buy alcohol. "It wasn't uncommon for me to wake up naked in a strange bed, next to a strange woman whose name I didn't know," he says with a hearty laugh. And while everyone else in the room is greatly amused by the speaker's stories, I am not; as a result, I find myself feeling like an outsider, yet again.

Feeling agitated about not having the same reaction as everyone else, I excuse myself and go to find an on-duty counselor. I'm in luck that night since Mike is on-call. Heavy-set and nearly bald, Mike wears wire-framed eyeglasses that give him the appearance of being scholarly.

"I didn't relate to one thing the speaker was saying!" I say with a judgmental scowl. "His stories weren't funny at all and they revealed a total lack of integrity. I didn't do any of the things he talked about; I never cheated or lied or stole or prostituted myself for clonazepam," I tell him.

"You don't have to identify with every speaker," Mike says, "Remember, you're here to find your own way: To listen to your body and find your own truth. Take what works for you and leave the rest behind."

I appreciate Mike's words, and his message about listening to my own intuition resonates with me.

Part way through the program, Yellow Group members are given a homework assignment to complete in the Art Room: a light, bright space, where residents are allowed to come and go freely. The assignment is called The Three Circles, and it is supposed to help us identify our own unique behaviors that promote or endanger our sobriety. As the art teacher hands us each a large piece of paper that she tears off a roll, I glom onto the idea of creating a personal piece of artwork to look at when I am back home in Rochester to remind me about what I have learned at The Meadows and to help me access the tools I have to handle difficult situations, which will inevitably arise.

That night, I spend several hours in the studio painting an enormous yellow orb with a dark black core. When we get to group the next day, I'm a little embarrassed when I see how elaborate my Recovery Circle is compared to what everyone else has done, but the counselor and the members of my group are enthusiastic about what I've painted.

Though I've always been a creative person, I've never been singled out for being particularly artistic, so it is a complete surprise when my new friend Bradley pulls me aside after a group therapy session to ask if he can buy my Recovery Circle before he leaves The Meadows. "It's gorgeous," he says. "I'd totally frame it and hang it in my house." It's been a long time since I've received any kind of positive feedback, and I respond to Bradley's kind words of praise with suspicion. I feel like he wants something more from me than art, and I don't know how to handle the situation. That evening, instead of attending the 12-Step meeting, I meet with a counselor.

"Have you always had difficulty recognizing your own strengths and accepting compliments?" he asks.

"I don't know," I say. "I guess I feel like people only compliment me when they want something."

It is an epiphany of sorts for me to realize that much of my negative self-talk started after marriage. Whenever there is a gathering with my husband's family, I end up feeling diminished in one way or another. I say the wrong thing to my sister-in-law; my matzo balls are too salty; no one likes my ideas about how to handle the holidays; I spend too much time with my nieces and nephews. After years of being shut down by my husband and his family, I no longer believe in my ideas or myself.

"Look, you're smart, you're talented, and you're easy on the eyes," my counselor says. "People love to tear down folks who appear to have it all."

"But I don't have it all," I insist.

"Of course you don't," he says. "No one does. But to the outside world, it certainly appears that you do."

Up until this moment, it has never occurred to me that people might look at me and find me intimidating. I think about how I've spent half my life comparing myself to other people, always coming up short. The counselors at The Meadows offer me an oppositional worldview, one that works against the negative thought-loop that seems to play on continuous repeat in my head. When I focus too much on my weaknesses, the counselors remind me of my strengths. They remind me that I am a college graduate, that I have a master's degree and a teaching degree. They remind me that I am a human being, that I am not too much. That, in fact, I am enough just the way I am.

• • •

Prior to the third week of the program, I call my husband and ask him if he might be interested in coming to Arizona to participate in Family Week for five days of intensive marriage counseling. It has been illuminating for me to understand how my most maladaptive behaviors stem from layers of unprocessed past traumas. I look at how I had been taught to prioritize other people's comfort over my own, how I was taught to keep silent and keep secrets. I can see, now, that staying quiet has not served me well. It is my hope that my husband will be willing to look at his family of origin, explore his own maladaptive coping skills within our own relationship, so we can begin the healing process together.

"If you sign me out, I'll be allowed to leave campus and we can spend some time alone together," I tell him. "I can even spend the night in your hotel room with you… if you want."

Derek is not at all enthusiastic about coming to Arizona, and when I tell my counselor that my husband doesn't want to miss work or cut into his vacation time, someone from the Meadows calls to explain to him about the benefits of attending the program, and he is persuaded to make the trip.

Prior to the arrival of our spouses, residents do a fair amount of preparation. The Yellow Group is divided into smaller sub-groups, and Marni, Peter, Bradley and I learn that – along with two marriage counselors, we will all be present during each other's therapy sessions with our respective spouses. We carefully craft the five most important points we wish to address with our family members, and tour the space where the meeting will take place. "In the best cases, this collaborative experience brings families closer together," our counselor says.

It's unseasonably hot that first week in March, with temperatures soaring above eighty-five degrees. I sort through my clean clothes, trying to cobble together some kind of attractive outfit in which to meet my husband and finally settling on a pair of cropped black yoga pants and a tee shirt borrowed from another patient.

A few days later, Derek shows up at The Meadows wearing khaki pants and a button-down shirt. Despite his casual office attire, he looks nervous, and I find myself wanting to reassure him. We have been instructed to keep the conversations light and keep our hands to ourselves, and so I do. I tour Derek around the campus and introduce him to my new friends, and after a short visit, he returns to his hotel a few miles away while I go to the dining room for dinner.

For two days, our little group travels together, attending lectures and activities. Always a model student, Derek is open-minded and genuinely interested in what he is hearing. While he is fascinated by the clinical aspects of the experience and enjoys learning about trauma and disease, he is not particularly present with me as a husband. "You needed this a long time ago," he whispers to me during a lecture on attachment theory.

Each day, after lunch, members of the Yellow Group and our spouses retire to a sterile white classroom on the second floor of one of the buildings on the Meadows' campus. Peter's girlfriend and Bradley's wife do not choose to attend Family Week, and the two men sit side by side in metal chairs as we listen to each other share the most intimate details of our relationships.

When it is finally our turn to share, Derek and I sit facing each other in chairs set about four feet apart. While Derek answers all my questions, calmly and coolly, and without emotion, I save my most difficult topic for last – it is a statement about the lack of physical intimacy in our marriage, which has been a core issue from the beginning of our relationship.

"When I make repeated requests for physical intimacy -- and you choose to go golfing, or ride your bike, or watch television, what I make up about that is that you don't want to be with me, that you think I'm unattractive – and about that I feel sad and confused and scared."

Tears roll down my cheeks. It is incredibly hard for me to make myself vulnerable in this way, to speak about the rejection I've endured for nearly two decades, and it feels like forever before my husband responds.

Derek rocks back in his chair and puts one hand on the top of his head. "I don't see how I can do anything better than I'm doing it now," he says.

Upon hearing my husband's answer, Bradley stands up and points at my husband. "That's fucked up!" he shouts, kicking over his chair. I know he's hurt that his wife has opted not to attend any family therapy sessions, and he storms out of the session.

The two counselors look at each other and, without exchanging a word, one of them gets up and leaves the room, ostensibly to go after Bradley, while the other stays in his chair to help us finish out our session.

My counselor pointedly asks my husband if he can agree to provide me with more physical and emotional intimacy than he previously has, but Derek has had enough. That afternoon, Derek informs me he is going back to Rochester. "I've already been gone too long," he explains.

When he leaves the next morning, I'm so overcome with grief that I cannot speak. For weeks, I've watched couples reconcile massive relational issues around addiction, adultery and theft. The process has been transformative for so many people. I had been hopeful the same might be true for us.

That night, I go to the art room, scribbling profanity all over an abandoned canvas before covering it with different shades of acrylic paint. While the paint is wet, I scratch tiny X's into the paint with the pointy end of my paintbrush. The end result is far from pretty, but it feels good to make these marks. It's the first time that I intentionally use art as a coping mechanism.

"That technique you're using is called 'tachisme'," the art therapist says, pointing at my canvas. "All those drips and blobs, the scribbling, the scratching: it's very cool."

I can barely see the art therapist through my tears. I didn't know there was a name for what I was doing. I was simply painting intuitively, from the gut, without any knowledge that I was using a specific technique.

During my final week in Wickenburg, I meet with an Outtake Specialist to discuss my plans upon leaving The Meadows – specifically where I will be going, how I will get there, and what kind of support I will have in place. I know that my husband has purchased a plane ticket back to Rochester for me and that he will pick me up from the airport. Outside of that, I don't know much else. The counselor hands me a printout of 12-Step meetings in my area and gives me a hug.

My last morning in Arizona, I'm up before the sun. My suitcase feels heavy as I drag it up the path to the main building. Upon signing the requisite discharge papers, a nurse returns my nail clippers and my cellphone to me. A short while later, a rusty taxicab arrives to shuttle me to the Phoenix International Airport, about an hour away. Midway through the trip, a single hot-air balloon appears from out of nowhere, hovering over the top of the jagged red rocks. I watch the balloon with great interest as it slowly gains altitude before dropping a few feet. As it surges and sags, I remember something my Meadows' counselor once told me. "Healing is not linear," he said. "Some days it's one step forward and two steps back."

With my Recovery Circle rolled up inside a tube and resting on my lap, I feel a little like that balloon – a bit floaty and uncertain about what lies ahead, but doing it anyway.

CHAPTER 20
HOMECOMING

After forty-five days in rehab, I return to Rochester. It's April now, and the earliest spring flowers are pushing up through the grass. It's strange to see so much green after having been in the red Arizona desert for over a month. Even the sky looks different.

Upon my return, I make an appointment with Dr. Halligan to discuss my experience in Arizona and to discuss the medications I've been taking at The Meadows. "Seroquel is a nasty drug," she says, and promptly changes me to a combination of Zyprexa (olanzapine) and Lithium Carbonate. The moment I come off the Seroquel, an old symptom that had gone away – tardive dyskinesia -- comes back. Dr. Halligan assures me that it will go away in time, and thankfully, she is right.

After seeing Dr. Halligan, I call Renee to let her know what's been going on.

"I've been worried about you," she says. "How are you doing?"

I tell her about my time in Arizona, what I learned, and fill her in about some of the people I met. I explain that I'm still very cognitively scrambled and worried that my brain will never heal. "If I get into trouble here, can I come back to your house?" I ask.

"Absolutely," she says without hesitation. "Just give me a call if you need me."

• • •

For the next ten months, Derek and I attend extensive marriage counseling. We try three different therapists before landing with one he likes. Bruce's office is cozy and packed with books and art. The couch is lumpy and uncomfortable, but Bruce is warm and personable. He listens to both of us and tries to be impartial. During one of our sessions, I express interest in procuring a studio space in a local warehouse that has been subdivided into small units.

I do extensive research and learn that the smallest studio will cost just over $250 per month, including renter's insurance, but my husband is adamant that I can continue to make art at home and offers to set up space for me in the basement. "We can put a tarp over the rug . . ." Derek insists. " . . . And you can carry water down from the kitchen."

From my standpoint, the entire discussion is ridiculous. Our finished basement with its expensive carpet and wheat colored walls was designed to be a hangout for our son and his friends. I don't want to take that space away from him, and it wasn't designed with my creative needs in mind.

"I'd prefer to be with a community of other artists," I tell him. "I think I'll eventually be able to make enough money to break even on the rent."

Derek tells me that my having a private studio isn't feasible and suggests I submit to him a business plan to prove that I will be able to make a profit on my proposed business venture. "Otherwise, it's just not worth it," he says.

Derek's lack of support takes my breath away. I've always encouraged his goals and dreams, and I'm shocked to learn that he is unwilling to support me in mine, and I am finally seeing it for the first time.

With Bruce's help, we manage to hash out a host of simple things, but when we begin to address our more complicated underlying intimacy issues, it's clear my husband feels attacked. At the end of one particularly difficult session, Derek storms out of Bruce's office, leaving me there alone.

"What do I do now?" I ask.

Without missing a beat, Bruce puts both his hands on my shoulders. "You get a divorce!" he says, shaking me gently.

Up until this moment, I've never considered divorce as a viable option. Raised in a conservative, Jewish family, I'd been taught to believe that when a couple gets married, their souls become one; that marriage is like a spiritual operation that takes separate beings and fuses them into a new whole. To religious Jews, divorce is the equivalent of a spiritual amputation, severing one part of the united soul from the other. Just as a doctor would do everything to avoid amputating a limb, I have been taught that it is imperative to do everything possible to avoid divorce. To me, marriage is forever. There is no Plan B.

After that session in Bruce's office, I am very upset. Things are tense at home, and I call Renee to tell her I'm feeling lost. "I feel like Dorothy from The Wizard of Oz. It's like I've landed in this strange new place where nothing is familiar. I don't know where I am or what to do."

There is a long pause on the other end of the phone. “I think you know what to do,” Renee says. “You have everything you need. Just wait for the next instruction.”

• • •

One cold night in January 2015, I stay up late to paint. Outside, the wind is howling and the temperatures plummet to below freezing. While I am standing in the kitchen, I hear a voice. It is the same Voice of deep knowing that I have heard many times before. *You’ve Got to Go*, it says.

I put my hands over both my ears in an attempt to silence the sound.

You’ve Got to Go.

Glancing at the clock, I notice the late hour and rationalize that my auditory hallucination is due to a lack of sleep. But at the same time, I have a new understanding of this Voice – one that I’ve gained as a result of the time I spent with Renee and my time spent at The Meadows. It is my own Deepest Intuition, the Voice of my Highest Self, trying to share some wisdom with me. Though I want to ignore the Voice, I realize The Universe is commanding me to do something and, at this point in my journey, I know better than to attempt to override it for long.

PART THREE

BUTTERFLY

CHAPTER 21
LETTING GO

In February of 2015, the snow is coming down hard as I drive home from yet another appointment with my therapist. The roads are icy, and I decide to pull over and wait for visibility to improve before I drive further. Suddenly, I notice an apartment building that I've never seen before. A large purple flag flapping in the wind reads VACANCY, and I feel compelled to stop to take a look. The landlord introduces me to the doorman, and then takes me up the elevator to show me a bright, clean, two-bedroom apartment on the fourth floor.

As he opens a door to show me the closet in the master bedroom, the landlord tilts his head at me. "You realize you're about thirty years younger than the youngest tenant in this building, right?" the landlord says. "I want to be transparent about that."

I realize the landlord is trying his best to inform me about the realities of life in his building, and I understand, also, that though I look like a regular woman in her mid-forties, the reality is that during this period in my life, I feel and behave more like a woman in her seventies or eighties. I've not worn makeup or had a haircut in over a year. No longer focused on the opinions of others, I find myself seeking solitude. I am gentle with myself and unapologetic about my seemingly endless need to rest. I'm going through an experience that is shaping me into something new, and I am being given a strange, new wisdom that I never wanted but that I am willing to share with anyone who might be willing to listen.

It isn't hard for me to imagine myself living in this building. In fact, I feel confident that I will fit in quite nicely.

That night, when Derek comes home from work, I tell him about the apartment I went to see earlier in the day, adding that I would like to take it. To his credit, Derek meets me back at the building the next day. He wants to confirm that the apartment will be safe and comfortable, not only for me, but also for our son.

"Are you sure you want to do this?" he asks.

"No," I tell him, "But something is forcing me to do it. I feel like if I don't do this, I'll die."

While I'm certain that Derek is positively perplexed during this period, he agrees to support me financially while we are living separately, and I am grateful to him for this, as I am still very disabled from my too rapid-taper several years earlier. Never for one minute did I think our separation would become a permanent arrangement. I truly believed that I was simply taking time to take care of myself without the added pressure of taking care of our home and our family.

The transition from my large, elegant home to a building filled with aging seniors, while necessary, is not easy. It takes weeks for me to collect boxes to pack up my clothes, toiletries and art supplies. I take very little furniture – a bed, a dresser, and a few tables.

On my first night in the apartment, my upstairs neighbors' toilet overflows causing brown, bilgy water to rain down from the overhead light fixture, saturating my bedroom carpet. In the past, my husband would've been the one to handle household repairs of this nature. Since I haven't been in the building long enough to meet the superintendent, I haven't any idea what to do. My closest girlfriend comes over and helps me to strategically place pots and pans to collect the raining toilet water until several hours later when the building manager is able to show up.

That night – and for many weeks after -- I find myself doubting myself for listening to The Voice that instructed me to leave everything I've ever known. But as time goes on, I appreciate the fact that the apartment affords me the opportunity to be responsible for no one else other than myself. I unpack my clothes and my dishes, and I create an area in my apartment where I can sit and make art, which I do constantly.

Shortly after I move into the apartment, Derek and I procure lawyers and work collaboratively to try to create the best situation for everyone involved. Eventually, we sit down together to explain to our son about what is happening to our family unit.

"I can't say I'm surprised," Cal says. "Now I'll be just like all my friends whose parents are divorced."

His proclamation makes me sad.

At this point, I've lost nearly two years with Cal, who is now a sophomore in high school. Cal's academics are important to him and, because he is enrolled in many Honors and Advanced Placement classes, he spends hours holed up studying in his new bedroom in my apartment. Occasionally, I'm able to convince him to come out and play a board game with me and, once or twice, we dust off the Nerf guns and chase each other up and down the building stairwells for a competitive game of tag. I hate having my son with me only 50% of the time, and

I'm always sad on Sunday nights when he returns to his father's house.

Around this time, a friend gives me an old fish-tank along with all the fixings: rocks, plastic plants, and a bubbler. I purchase two bubble-eye goldfish, both of which promptly die after about a week in my apartment. The loss feels weirdly symbolic to me, and I'm forced to accept the fact that I'm still very sick and that I can hardly take care of myself, much less, another living thing. Filled with a deep sense of guilt and shame for being unable to do things that were at one time second nature to me, it's hard to admit that I simply don't have the physical energy or the mental resources to devote to anyone or anything beyond my own basic survival.

Months pass, and I become friendly with the people in my building. The residents on the fourth floor are particularly kind. Nearly everyone is over seventy years old, and collectively, they adopt me, buoying me up and looking out for me. I learn the rhythm of the building and the people behind the doors. One of my neighbors plays his trombone every day at 3PM, and another neighbor plays the piano. I visit the sparsely appointed workout room in the basement, and I make a brief appearance at the building book club. I keep my door open all day long, and my neighbors bring me all sorts of baked goods. I learn about their families -- the people they love and long for. We share joys and sorrows, talk about local news stories of interest, and complain about politics and the weather.

Outside of my parents and my son, I have few visitors. The truth is I am in no condition to entertain. Nearly three years after weaning off clonazepam, I still suffer from involuntary muscle spasms and jerky, throwing movements of my head and extremities, which are physically exhausting. Though some of my symptoms have disappeared at this point, new ones have come to take their place, the worst of which is the akathisia, best described as a never-ending inner restlessness. For me, this non-stop inner vibration both wears me out and makes it hard to sit still. Because I am so physically uncomfortable, I spend many hours alone in my apartment, moving from bed to couch. When I am not resting, I spend most of my time on my computer connecting with other people who have been similarly injured by pharmaceuticals. I continue to paint, meditate and practice my breath work.

It is both an incredibly intense and simultaneously dull existence – but at this point, I have accepted that this is the way my life is going to be and my only goal is to get up each morning and make it through another day.

During this period, I continue my weekly therapy sessions with Vickijo, and we delve into the life events that helped shape my view of the world and my place in it. While I was taking clonazepam, I'd had different types of talk therapy, but it is only now that I am off the drug that I am able to remember and process the events of my past. Over the course of the hundreds of hours I spend sitting on Vickijo's white couch, she helps me to realize that for much of my life, I've made unhealthy choices in relationships, that I've been protecting people who, in reality, have treated me poorly and/or have not always had my best interests at heart. Vickijo helps me deconstruct and re-contextualize the impact of physical and emotional abuse that I endured while growing up. We explore early messaging that I learned from my family and from my religious tradition, as well as messages I absorbed as a female growing up in the United States during the 1970s and 1980s. We also address sexual trauma I experienced as a teenager.

Vickijo explains to me some of the problems that existed within my marriage, how some people use the silent treatment as a way to exert power over someone else or to create emotional distance. I think about how my husband would disappear whenever I tried to address the intimacy issues in our marriage. "When people are uncomfortable discussing a topic," Vickijo says, "it is generally easier for them to avoid the conversation entirely. You may have picked a partner who never raged at you, but the silent treatment can be abusive too."

And suddenly, I see it: How my husband and – in fact, most of his family -- made me feel like we were not on the same team, but rather that I was the enemy, standing on the other side of a locked door. I see how I took that first pill to fit in, to tamp down the edges of my personality that felt more, saw more and questioned more than those around me. I realize how the clonazepam allowed me to maintain status quo by numbing me to those uncomfortable feelings of rejection, of seeing and saying "too much," more than what was comfortable or convenient for others.

Having a therapist share an alternative worldview of the events that took place during the course of my life is simultaneously liberating and devastating. "It's hard to believe it, I know, but these people loved you. They were doing the best that they could at the time with the information and skills they had," Vickijo says. "And you were doing the best you could do, too. You didn't know how to share your feelings. You may have thought you were communicating, but nobody was really communicating honestly with each other."

While I learn to hold several contradictory and competing ideas in my head at the same time, I truly feel I am in a period of in-between. Neither as sick as I once was, but far from being well, I think of myself as an emerging butterfly that has just started to crack its chrysalis. Though I know I am no longer a caterpillar, I have no idea of what my new life is going to look like. I remind myself that during the darkest days of winter, when it feels like spring will never come again, somehow it always does. Somehow after those cold, dark nights, the light feels extra bright and so very welcome.

To pass the time, I create a routine for myself, a kind of unconventional curriculum. In the mornings, immediately upon waking, I make my bed, do a little restorative yoga, and practice tapping, using the Emotional Freedom Technique. I take a long shower, dress, and try to accomplish one thing on my to-do list. Things that used to be effortless -- like paying a bill, going to the grocery store, or getting my car serviced -- are still difficult endeavors for me, but I am doing better than I was three years earlier when I was essentially bedridden.

There was a time in my life when I would have been one of the first to roll my eyes at someone claiming to have special environmental sensitivities. Now, after suffering from this neurological injury, I'm more sensitive to different environmental stimuli, including chemicals found in cleaning products, perfumes and dyes. Foods that have never bothered me before cause my symptoms to flare. In response to the onset of these new sensitivities, I adjust my diet so that I eat only whole foods, which is to say no dairy, no gluten, no red meat, no MSG, and very little processed sugar. After lunch, I listen to YouTube meditations and inspirational podcasts by well-recognized spiritual leaders. During the week, I watch very little television, but I never miss *Oprah's Super Soul Sunday* and I find each interview more compelling than the last since they are filled with hopeful stories about overcoming trauma and spiritual transformation.

On alternating weeks, when my son comes to stay with me in my apartment, I work hard to prepare meals that will appeal to him. My cognition is still so impaired that fixing food presents a real challenge. Walking into the kitchen each time is like walking into a stranger's kitchen. I can't remember where I have put this or that. Though I once considered myself a good cook with a broad repertoire of recipes I could call upon at a moment's notice, it is disheartening to experience the feeling of having forgotten how to prepare even the most basic recipes.

While divorce always creates challenges in family dynamics, the fact that I am still experiencing physical symptoms of protracted benzodiazepine withdrawal amplifies the situation. My ex-husband and I are generally on the same page in terms of co-parenting; however, there are certain areas in which we have different expectations. Because I am easily fatigued, I try to stay on top of small household tasks, but when Cal comes to stay with me for his week, the dishes pile up and there is always more laundry to do, and when I ask him to help, he pushes back in the way teenagers do. "At home Dad does the dishes," he argues.

"I know," I say. "I need a little extra help."

Usually, Cal rolls his eyes and acquiesces, but sometimes he fights with me, which leaves me feeling frazzled for days. It's upsetting not to be able to do simple things to make his life easier, but I use the skills I learned at The Meadows to keep my expectations in check, and I settle for doing my best, even when my best doesn't feel anywhere near good enough.

As I continue to heal from my invisible injury, I begin to read about what stress does to our bodies and our brains. I meet people who have suffered traumatic brain injuries and we compare notes about our symptomology. I learn that brain injuries can cause a disruption in time perception; they can impact one's appetite, interfere with cognition and concentration. I read that brain injuries can cause insomnia, gastrointestinal unrest, reproductive problems and fatigue. They can sap sexual desire and tissue repair.

I begin to realize that coming off of clonazepam too quickly is essentially like being chemically concussed, and I seek out holistic treatments that might help to accelerate the healing process. I try acupuncture, detoxifying foot soaks, and aromatherapy as part of my routine. Some of these treatments are effective, while others do very little to alleviate symptoms.

I am fortunate to have ample financial resources available so that I can rest and focus solely on healing my injured central nervous system. Most people do not have that luxury and, unfortunately, insurance companies do not yet recognize how long it takes to heal from this type of iatrogenic injury. In fact, to date, they still do not recognize protracted withdrawal as being associated with the cessation of benzodiazepines.

With the help of my divorce lawyer, I'm fortunate to negotiate a settlement that allows me to continue to hold health insurance, which helps to offset some of the expenses associated with many of these unconventional treatments. And while studies show there is no evidence to support that these alternative therapies shorten the duration of damage caused by benzodiazepines, they feel good and serve as a good distraction for me. Distraction during benzo withdrawal is essential and researching alternative therapies provides me with something to focus on besides my physical pain.

CHAPTER 22
BECOMING

May of 2015 brings beautiful weather, with temperatures that climb up to nearly ninety degrees. While out on my daily walk, I meet a woman who tells me she works as a part-time bus driver for the Rochester City School District.

The two of us walk to a local grocery store where we share lunch. In between bites of my salad, I tell her about the nature of my injury and what I'm going through. I'm surprised by how supportive Lola is. She believes me when I tell her about my long list of somatic symptoms that began upon the cessation of clonazepam nearly three years earlier.

"I know a lot of people who have been injured by drugs," she says, crumpling up her sandwich wrapper. "Heroin is a bitch, but benzos are worse."

Doubted for years by medical professionals and told my experience with protracted benzodiazepine syndrome – indeed, my entire reality – was "not possible, not credible and evidence of severe mental illness," I feel validated when Lola, a stranger, understands what I am going through better than any doctor, friend or family member has over the last three years.

When we finish eating and right before we part ways, I ask Lola if I can take her photograph. "I'd like to paint your portrait," I say.

"Are you an artist?" she asks.

"Kind of," I say, "I like to paint."

Lola laughs and gives me permission.

That evening, I look at the photograph on my camera and sketch a black and white line drawing of a woman who looks absolutely nothing like Lola. When I post the finished painting on Facebook and explain the story behind it, I am met with a deluge of positive responses. "You should ask other people if you can paint their portraits," someone suggests.

I lock into this idea, and the next time I log into Facebook, I announce that I'm looking for eighteen female volunteers to participate in a unique opportunity that I call *The State of Undress Project***.** To be part of my project, participants have to be able to articulate an obstacle they have overcome (or that they are actively working on) and be willing to frame that particular challenge as a strength.

The next morning, when I check my email, I am surprised to see that several responses are waiting for me, compete with photos. For the first time in a long time, I am filled with a sense of purpose, and I paint day and night. On Monday nights, I attend an open figure drawing class in the studio of a prominent local artist to work on my technique, and I meet a host of creative people who share my passion for making art.

By October 2015, with the help of Dr. Halligan, I manage to wean off all the additional psychiatric drugs I was prescribed while in rehab in Arizona. This was no small feat. Over a fifteen-year period, I was on and off an array of prescription psychotropic medications including Prozac, Zoloft, Celexa, Buspar, Lamictal, Klonopin, Equatro, Valium, Seroquel, Risperdone, Zyprexa, Olanzipine, Quetiapine, Trazadone, Lithium and Latuda. All told, I ingested thousands of pills and paid thousands of dollars in co-payments to my insurance company, but the biggest price I paid is not one that can be easily measured. I was told psychiatric drugs would make me well, when – in reality – they caused me lose my connection to my true self and, as a result, become very, very sick.

"You've done it!" Dr. Halligan says at our last appointment.

"Yes," I say, giving her a quick hug. "And now I'm firing your ass."

Dr. Halligan laughs good-naturedly at my comment. Though she has been nothing but helpful to me throughout my tapers, at this point, I've decided psychiatry is the enemy, and the further away I get from the drugs, the better I feel. Dr. Halligan seems to understand my feelings, and she assures me that she doesn't take my comment personally. In fact, she celebrates the fact that I have managed to extricate myself from psychiatric medication.

• • •

A month later, on a Friday night, a girl friend convinces me to dress up so we can enjoy a nice meal and then go to The Hungerford Building, a gritty, old brick building in the city of Rochester. Once a major manufacturing plant, the owner of the building was a visionary who transformed the enormous industrial space into individual studios of varying sizes, hoping to attract a vibrant community of artists, craftspeople and small business owners. Though I've lived in Rochester for over twenty-five years, I'm stunned that something like The Hungerford Building exists and I'd never even heard mention of it before.

That night, while exploring the Hungerford, I meet a local textile artist who offers me an opportunity to sublet a little gallery space inside her studio, and right before my 49th birthday in the fall of 2016, I begin to show my artwork in public. It is during one of my First Friday exhibitions that I meet a web designer who agrees to help me set up a website where I can sell my original artwork as well as printed reproductions. Investing in myself is a terrifying endeavor, but I start doing shows and festivals to offset the costs associated with the upkeep of the website.

Each month, I manage to meet someone new. I love connecting with other people, listening to their stories, and figuring out how we might be able to collaborate. At one of my art shows, I get to talking with a woman who tells me I might benefit from another kind of noninvasive bodywork – Myofascial Release (MR), an alternative therapy useful for treating skeletal muscle immobility and pain by relaxing contracted muscles, improving blood, oxygen, and lymphatic circulation, and stimulating the stretch reflex in muscles.

Prior to my brain injury, I may have expressed interest in alternative therapies, but I would not have followed through to pursue these treatments because of messaging I had received both from my parents and my ex-husband who believed alternative therapies to be the work of snake-oil salesmen. Now, however, I am more than open to people and modalities that others might consider to be New Age, so I take the name of the person who is being recommended to me, and the next day, I make the call.

CHAPTER 23
HEALING

Maria's office is small and, with the exception of the bubbling waterfall in the middle of her waiting area, decorated in a minimalistic manner. During my first 60-minute session, Maria spends a lot of time on my occipital ridge, the region at the back of the neck that connects the base of the skull to the spine. With slow and deliberate movements, she uses varying pressure ranging from extremely light to very deep, which she holds for up to ninety seconds, after which time the muscle she is working on seems to relax.

While Maria works on my head and neck during our first MR session, a weird taste floods my mouth. "Yuck," I say, smacking my lips. "I taste metal."

Maria is not surprised. "Sometimes people experience a metallic taste in their mouth when they are detoxing heavy metals," she says. "Have you ever been tested for lead or mercury?"

Maria's inquiry leads me to speak to my doctor about doing some more specific laboratory testing for iron, lead, magnesium and a host of twelve other heavy metals, and I am directed to a company in Illinois that offers an at-home test to detect these toxins in one's urine. A few weeks later, the test results reveal that I am off the charts for mercury, lead and chromium, and I am prescribed DMSA (2-3 dimercaptosuccinic acid), a chelation agent commonly used to help remove heavy metals from the body.

At this point, I find a new physician, one who practices Integrative Medicine. She encourages me to add several supplements to my diet, as she believes consuming them will go a long way toward ridding my body of heavy metals in the future. She tells me to add Hawaiian Spirulina and Atlantic Dulse to my daily smoothie. Apparently, in addition to mercury, this edible seaweed binds to lead, aluminum, copper, cadmium, and nickel. She encourages me to try to consume at least two or three of these supplements every day. I continue to experience so many strange body symptoms which I have cross-referenced with other benzodiazepine sufferers that I am reluctant to seek help from Western doctors; however, I've been experiencing terrible dental pain, which I learn is a common symptom associated with benzodiazepine withdrawal. After seeing a dentist, I'm diagnosed with Burning Mouth Syndrome, a painful condition characterized by a scalding sensation on the tongue, lips, palate, or throughout the mouth that can persist for months or years.

At certain times, my dental pain is so severe that it literally brings me to my knees. My dentist notes that I have a mouth filled with deteriorating mercury fillings, and he recommends that I have them removed, which I do. Within a week, the pain in my face noticeably decreases by about 50% so I only feel a slight residual tingle on the left side of my mouth.

• • •

Time passes, and I continue to run through my routines. I meet with various holistic practitioners and research many non-traditional modalities of healing. I invest in a series of ionic foot soaks, which supposedly remove heavy metal toxins through the feet. I try an aggressive chelation treatment, the results of which reveal that I have abnormally high levels of lead, mercury and other metals in my urine. I read an article that suggests infrared light can be useful as part of a heavy-metal detoxification protocol, and that the treatment may also improve the circulation of oxygen-rich blood in the body, promoting faster healing of deep tissues and relieving pain. At this point in my journey, I am open to nearly anything, and I begin to regularly see a woman who uses a special deep infrared wand all over my body in an effort to promote cell regeneration and regrowth.

Healing from the damage caused by taking a benzodiazepine doesn't happen in a linear fashion. It's not like recovering from the flu – each day getting a bit better after the height of infection. Healing comes in what is referred to in the benzodiazepine community as "windows" and "waves." Windows are times when one's symptoms are milder, more manageable, or non-existent. This experience can last for a few hours, days, weeks or even longer. Waves are times when one's symptoms increase in severity or new symptoms appear after a period of improvement. What causes a wave to occur is unknown and it seems to differ from person to person. Some people attribute waves to something they ate or drank but, in truth, there is no way to pinpoint the cause and these cycles are unpredictable. Where some people experience a gradual loosening of symptoms, this is not my experience.

After several Myofascial Release sessions with Maria, I sit up from the table, stunned to notice that I do not have any somatic symptoms at all. For thirty months, I can detect no decrease or change in my daily symptoms, but on this day, for the first time in years, my head does not feel like it is being pulled or squeezed, neither do I the feel chronic rocking dizziness – that unpleasant feeling of being on a boat in the middle of a storm. For one hour, my akathisia is completely gone, and I feel clear-headed.

It is difficult to express how impactful this moment is for me: experiencing my first "window" truly restores my hope, and I adopt the optimistic belief that if I can enjoy one symptom-free hour that I can eventually enjoy two symptom-free hours – and that, one day, the nightmare that is benzodiazepine withdrawal will eventually end.

And, over time, that is exactly what begins to happen. I reach a point in my healing where I am able to coexist with my symptoms; they are still present and extremely exhausting, but I no longer feel disabled. By this time, I am able to do more and I begin to make more reliable social plans with people. I still feel like everyone can tell how cognitively impaired I am by looking at me, but this does not seem to be the case. When I look in the mirror, I no longer look like a crone. My complexion brightens, my hair and fingernails grow back long and strong, and my muscle tone improves.

I'm convinced that it is a combination of good nutrition, right thinking, exercise, quality rest, and time that helps me to get better. Between my deep breathing techniques, my long walks in nature, the paintings I make, the writing I do in my gratitude journal, the DBT, the bodywork, the gluten free diet: all of it seems to have a cumulative effect. Though I am still very sick, I am able to set small goals for myself and I try to achieve these goals each day.

By January 2016, I take a part time job at a local community college working twelve hours a week as a Tutor in the Center for Academic Reading (CAR) to provide support to developmentally challenged students who need a little extra assistance. Though I'm fatigued at the end of each shift in the CAR, I am happy to be in the classroom and to be of service to others again.

CHAPTER 24
INTEGRATION

My desire for personal growth leads me to examine the myriad spiritual and philosophical ideas and practices in the world. I keep my mind open to unfamiliar options and explore the world of divination, auras, Reiki and sound baths. Soon after, I begin to experience a series of powerful coincidences, which I come to recognize as 'messages' or action steps from the Universe, which cannot (or should not) be ignored.

For a time, it seems that each new person with whom I meet and share my story has the same question. "Have you ever been to The Purple Door?" they all ask. Initially, I pay no heed to the question and simply say that I've never heard of the place. But one day, while I am out searching for a new queen-sized mattress, I strike up an easy conversation with a salesperson. Somehow, while we walk around the store, I end up telling him a little bit about my experience in Renée McLain's basement – about the voice I'd heard and the message I felt I'd been given by a Guiding Spirit.

"I assume you've been to The Purple Door then," he says. "Right?"

At this point, I'm looking up at the ceiling while lying on the umpteenth mattress, trying to discern how this particular bed feels against the small of my back as compared to the last. "You're probably the fifth or sixth person who's mentioned that place to me," I say, rolling over onto my side to face him. "I haven't been there, so tell me: What's the deal with this 'Purple Door'?"

The salesman looks around. He seems to be making sure that we are the only two people in the showroom within earshot. "It's a small place, not too far from here," he says. "You can meet with a psychic medium, get a tarot card reading or a palm reading; there are people who offer dream interpretations, and lots of other services for people who have had or are currently having some kind of metaphysical experience. If you've had a lot of people recommend it to you, it's probably time for you to check it out."

A day later, I find myself pulling into a tiny parking lot located off to the side of strip mall. After passing an authentic Indian restaurant and the United States Army Recruitment Office, I turn a corner and then I see it: an unassuming door painted a vibrant shade of purple.

Upon opening the door, I hear bells jingle to alert the staff of my arrival. The store smells like patchouli and there are crystals and decks of Tarot cards and all the kinds of things you would expect to find in a metaphysical gift shop. A woman with chin-length red hair is standing behind a glass counter. She is fussing with something when she looks up at me with a smile; but then, rather than saying anything to greet me, the woman covers her open mouth with her hand. "Omigosh!" she says dramatically. "You're here. I can't believe it!"

I look around, confused. *Certainly, she is talking to someone else and not to me*, I think.

But I am the only person in the store.

"Sue!" the woman says aloud. "Sue! You have to come out here!" Coming out from behind the glass display, she aims her voice toward a partially closed door, only a few steps away from where I'm standing. "The girl with the cat-eye glasses and the cowboy boots, she's here."

I have absolutely no idea what is happening, but I am, in fact, wearing cat-eye glasses and cowboy boots. At this point, a slim woman with brown hair and kind eyes materializes and joins the two of us at the center of the store. "Welcome," she says, extending a hand. "I've been waiting for you."

"Do you greet everyone like this?" I ask with skepticism.

"Hardly," the second woman laughs, and then explains to me how she has been having powerful dreams for several weeks, about a girl with ponytails and cat-eye glasses and cowboy boots. "You're even wearing a yellow sundress!" she says. "I hadn't remembered that detail until right now."

The two women exchange knowing looks.

"Why don't you come on back with me," Sue says, taking a few steps toward me. She touches me near my elbow. "I'd like to do a past-life regression with you."

Suddenly, I'm not sure what to do. I feel like I've made a terrible mistake, like the guy at the mattress store and these two women are in on some kind of scam. "I didn't bring any money," I announce. "I only just came in because a bunch of people suggested I take a look around."

"You don't have to pay a thing." Sue says, shaking her head definitively. "This is my gift to you. I have to do it."

Standing there, I look from one woman to the other. They are both smiling warmly at me, and I feel something strange and powerful. It is the feeling of sisterhood, and it is similar to the way I felt the day I met Renee McLain, when she found me sitting against the brick wall outside the medi-spa in Syracuse and brought me home to stay with her.

I remember Renee telling me that she had once had a past-life regression during which time she'd learned that she'd actually been a Queen at one time in history. I remember her saying that she came out of the experience feeling empowered.

I figure that I probably come from royalty, too. *Maybe I'm not a queen*, I think, *but maybe I'm a princess*.

What happens next is a bit of a blur.

First, Sue brings me into her tiny therapy room. She has me sit down and lean back into a comfortable chair, or maybe it is a couch or a recliner of some sort. I seem to remember the chair being burgundy, but maybe it was green or blue. Sue asks me take several deep breaths before leading me through a guided meditation during which time she asks me a series of questions. I'm completely aware and very relaxed. After a while, she asks me to describe where I am.

I see a damp, rather dark house with sooty windows and a dirty floor. Inside, there is a young woman inside wearing a long, heavy dress and shoes with stiff laces. Her green eyes look just like mine, but her loose curls are red and held in place by several mismatched combs. A man is there, too, surrounded by many children. I have a strong sense that these are not her children, though each of them seems to want something from her. She is a worker of some sort, perhaps an indentured servant or a nanny. When she opens her mouth to speak, someone strikes her with an open hand. Afterwards, she returns to the kitchen where she throws peeled potatoes into a pot of boiling water. I can feel how stuck she is: she wants more for herself, but she feels a sense of obligation and seems afraid to venture out of this house.

When there are no more images or memories around the house or the area, Sue guides me to move towards anything else I see, and I experience a powerful flashback of what appears to be the inside of a hull of a very old ship.

This time, I see a young woman, probably in her late teenage years or early twenties. As odd as it may sound, this time, I know the woman is, in fact, me. The first thing I notice about myself is that I have brown skin. The fact that I am a black woman doesn't faze me at all. This reality feels somehow familiar: like it is something I have always known about myself. I feel a terrible rocking sensation – a feeling of being seasick, but I can't get up to do anything about it. My ankles are shackled together with iron cuffs connected by a short bit of chain. Hungry and cold, I'm surrounded by dozens of other people, all of us sitting on the floor, atop of what looks and feels like loose hay. No one else is shackled except me. A woman I don't recognize sits beside me and lectures me about learning to "hold my tongue."

Somehow, I am transported back even further, to a tiny windowless room with a dusty floor.

It is very dark inside this space, and I feel inexplicably nervous in the sweltering heat. I cannot see myself, but I can hear myself breathing. A man enters, carrying some kind of light: a candle or a lantern. Adorned with many bracelets, he is wearing a bit of cloth, folded neatly and tied at the waist. Now I see myself. Bare-breasted and glancing nervously around the room, I am tugging at a chain connecting my ankle to what appears to be a slab of stone. I try to create as much space away from this man as I can, but I can't go very far. The man touches my shoulder. He tries to put his mouth on mine, but I turn my head away. There is an odd leap in time; I see myself curled into a fetal position, my right side pressing against the cold slab of stone. The man appears to be kneeling over me; he is pushing something sharp against my neck. When I ask him to let me go, he stabs me in the heart.

Suddenly, the faces of each woman – the girl with the red hair, the dark-skinned woman on the ship, and the bare-breasted slave-girl -- come rushing at me, almost as if pages in a flip book. I see my eyes reflected in other faces, too: the emaciated face of a woman locked inside of a gas chamber; the frightened face of an adolescent girl being restrained and made to open her legs; and finally, I see my own face. Stuck inside an invisible cage, an enclosure that only I can see, I stare up at the moon like a deranged animal.

Over the next half hour, Sue gently guides me back to her hypnosis room at The Purple Door. She hands me a plastic cup filled with water and instructs me to take small sips. After a little while, the two of us talk about what I saw, what I heard, and what I felt in each scenario. In each setting, the role of the woman is one of complete obedience, submission, and servitude – and this pattern feels sigificant to me.

"You've been a slave for many lifetimes," Sue says with authority. "This is probably the first lifetime you've ever been truly free."

Sue's insight cuts a little too close to the bone. After nearly twenty years of marriage, of looking out for someone else and being looked after, too, the idea of being "truly free" fills me with fear rather than exhilaration.

"You are here is to help usher in a new paradigm," Sue says. "People all over this world are waking up and stepping into their power. And yes, freedom can be scary, but I'm daring you to choose not to be scared. I'm daring you to live courageously, to let yourself explore and be drawn toward whatever you feel is right. When you do this, you will be living your truth."

At this point, I tell Sue my whole story. I tell her about my upbringing, about the multiple layers of trauma I have endured, the losses I have suffered. I tell her about how I was drugged for nearly a decade, and I share with her the horrifying details of benzodiazepine withdrawal. "I feel like I've been reborn and that I am having to start over from scratch," I tell her. "Nothing feels familiar to me anymore."

"You've been given a second chance," Sue says. She is playing with the cross around her neck and smiling at me. "What you do with it is up to you."

Having reached the end of the session, the two of us stand up. Sue and I embrace each other warmly, and she walks me outside to my car where I sit for a little while. It's a beautiful day, warm and sunny, and I keep my car door open so I can hear the birds chirping.

Opponents of past life-regression say people in hypnotic states are highly suggestible, and that may very well be true. All I know is that my experience with past-life regression gives me a way of understanding the strange physical sensations and blockages that I've been experiencing and which seem to transcend time. Upon leaving The Purple Door, I feel I possess a greater breadth and depth of understanding about where I am in my spiritual journey, about my purpose during this particular lifetime, and I lose any fear that I may have felt up until that point.

• • •

A few days after my session with Sue, things really start to click for me. I think back to how I learned about the Holocaust at a very young age, how I felt a strong affinity for the Jews who died or were killed in concentration camps. I couldn't have been older than six or seven years old, and soon after, my own personal experiences with anti-Semitism transformed what I'd previously only heard about in religious school (or read about in books or seen in movies) into a full sensory experience of my own. As a result of this early exposure to anti-Semitism, I developed a strong sense of social justice, often speaking out against anything that I experienced as racist, biased or derogatory in nature. I believed (and continue to believe) in speaking up because, to me, to not say something is to be complicit. It was easy for me to see what could happens when shame and fear collide – and how silence allows corrupt systems to take root and gain power.

In college, I was an outspoken challenger of the status quo. I received accolades for speaking out against all kinds of social injustice and, in 1989, I was the recipient of an academic award, given to one who encourages intellectual vitality in others and is outstanding in commitment to justice & action. However, the further I moved away from college and graduate school, immersing myself in my work as a teacher, the more I began to put everyone else's needs ahead of my own.

Upon marrying Derek and returning to New York State, I tried very hard to fit in to his family. From the outside, I'm sure everything seemed idyllic, but there were some unhealthy dynamics when it came to the way family members communicated with each other. There was a kind of fixed mindset about the way the family did things, which left little room for creativity, change or growth. On many occasions, I was explicitly asked to stay silent so as "not to make waves" or upset another member of the family. During this time, I internalized the message that it was okay to use my voice to take up for a cause that would benefit others, but it was not acceptable for me to speak with the same passion about my own needs: to do so would be selfish.

Over time, and without realizing it, I allowed myself to be silenced.

• • •

If I receive anything from my past-life regression it is that I must not be afraid to use my voice to speak out about what I know. I adopt the belief that I have made it through my benzodiazepine experience so that I can point out something that is broken within our current medical system, something that we are doing wrong, something that is injuring people. It is necessary for someone to point out these distortions so that things might be repaired—so that healing can occur and justice and trust may be restored.

As a result of my past-life regression experience, I make some immediate changes in my life, and I soon experience a series of amazing synchronicities. For example, after donating a small painting to a local art gallery, a stranger contacts me to tell me she purchased artwork and inquires if I have any other pieces similar to the one she has purchased. As it turns out, we have quite a bit in common, and she ends up inviting me to accompany her to a conference being held on Treasure Island, Florida. I feel completely safe with this woman, and I agree to go.

While I'm away, I spend every moment on the beach and experience a new sense of purpose around my new identity as an artist. I meet new people, careful to discern whose energy feels right and whose does not. I paint and write, and I gain confidence that I can navigate this strange, new world by myself. While experimenting with watercolor on the beach one morning, as part of my daily practice, a woman in a floppy hat approaches me. "I love your work," she says enthusiastically. "Do you do any festivals?"

"I've only been painting for just a few years," I tell her, offering her my sketchbook, filled with tiny original paintings. "I don't think I'm ready to do festivals yet."

The woman in the hat flips through the pages of my book and shifts her weight from one foot to another. "I'd like to buy your sketchpad," she says. "Would you take $100 for it?"

While I'm flattered, I politely refuse.

"Well," she says, handing me her business card. "If you ever decide to make prints, I'd be interested in purchasing some."

I consider this woman's interest in my art all that night and the following day. Using the breath-work I learned with Renee many years earlier, I lie down on the beach and put one hand on my heart and the other hand on my belly. With my eyes closed, I can feel the firm sand against my back and I can hear the seagulls squawking as they circle overhead. After taking several deep breaths, I ask the Universe for guidance. "What am I supposed to do next?" I say aloud.

At first, I hear only the ocean, and the sound of gulls screeching overhead. And then I hear it, an enigmatic message, coming through loud and clear.

There will be a Woman on the Airplane.

At the time, I have no idea what this means, but on my flight home from Florida, I end up sitting next to a retired potter. During our three hours in the air, she shows me photographs of her studio space and pictures of some of the ceramic vessels she'd designed over the course of her lifetime. Upon our descent into Rochester, she touches me on the knee. "Would you like to have my old, white festival tent?" she offers. "I'm not using it anymore."

A week later, after picking up her tent, I apply to a handful of local art shows. I buy several hundred dollars in art supplies, and I decide to invest in a significant amount of inventory, specifically high quality reproductions of my original work. It is an emotional and a financial investment in myself, the likes of which I have never made before. It feels scary and also exciting. I decide to focus on the adventure and leave the fear behind and, as soon as I commit to this new way of living, I experience a reduction in symptoms.

At forty-two months off clonazepam, I can tell I'm finally healing.

CHAPTER 25
REBORN

By June of 2017, I'm well enough to attend my son's high school graduation. It is a lovely day, and hundreds of proud parents pack themselves into the Gordon Fieldhouse on the Rochester Institute of Technology Campus to watch their children receive their diplomas.

Shortly after Cal walks across the stage, he ushers me off to the side and introduces me to one of his teachers, who shakes my hand warmly while looking confused. "I'm sorry," she says more to my son than to me. "I don't know that I've met you before."

It's a painful moment in which I'm forced to realize that I'm not the only one who has been profoundly impacted by the iatrogenic injury I suffered: my son, also, lost out on four years with his mother. If I want to, I can beat myself up for missing out on so much of my son's life. Luckily, Cal likes to remind me that the circumstances forced him to learn to take responsibility for his own self, and he believes he is better for it.

After Cal leaves Rochester to begin his first year in college in another state, I participate in my very first one-woman gallery show. Though I set an intention of painting eighteen figure studies, I end up painting seventy-five portraits in less than a year. The event is well attended and my story is written up in the local newspaper.

As a result of the publicity, many more people reach out to share their iatrogenic injury stories with me. It seems that nearly everyone I meet knows someone who has struggled with or lost his or her life due to prescription drugs.

• • •

At the time of this writing, eight years have passed since I experienced those terrible seizures in my kitchen. Today, nearly everything about my life is different. I'm a full-time artist, teacher, and writer with a strong anti-drug message. My cognitive function has slowly returned, and in 2018, I purchased a house and began to do all kinds of things that I never thought I would be able to do by myself.

Though Derek and I are no longer married, we've re-established a friendship, and we function nicely as a unit when it comes to co-parenting our son. It may interest some to know that while writing this book, I would sporadically call and ask my ex-husband questions because I wanted to make certain that my recollections were accurate. In nearly every case, Derek remembered events precisely as I did, often down to the minor details — and it has been fascinating for both of us to learn how the same situations elicited vastly different emotional reactions in each of us.

In the years since our divorce, Derek and I have been able to offer each other a little grace. He's explained to me that the pressure to be the full-time breadwinner for our family put tremendous stress on his shoulders, and he acknowledges that he prioritized his career over our relationship. He's apologized for not meeting my relational needs, and most importantly, Derek acknowledges that he interpreted my situational sadness as clinical depression, which — based on his training — was something to medicate.

I believe Derek when he says he didn't know about the dangers associated with benzodiazepines. As an ophthalmologist who does not write prescriptions for this class of drugs, it never occurred to him to question the prescription practice of another medical expert. He feels awful that I lost many years of good health due to drugs that harmed rather than helped. We have truly forgiven each other for our failures, for not knowing what we could not have known.

• • •

Since becoming a Certified Recovery Peer Advocate, I've spoken with hundreds of people who have also been injured by benzodiazepines, and I've come to the realization that each of us has been, in some way, subjected to an unusual combination of unfortunate events and false narratives that – taken together -- produced unusually bad results. Such a perfect storm is the result of a lifetime of grooming.

In the United States, we're raised from infancy to believe that people in white coats are "experts" who know what they're doing and have everything they need to make us feel better. We absorb information in carefully scripted commercials promising miraculous, safe, pharmaceutical solutions.

And while it's true that Western medicine has made many incredible advances, it's important to acknowledge that not every discovery or treatment works for every person.

People are being injured by prescription psychiatric medications. Some of us end up psychiatrized as a result of childhood abuse and trauma; others, after injury or illness. The common denominator, though, is that all of us were taught to look to an expert, someone outside of ourselves, to fix us. We all received the same messaging: if you're not feeling well, make an appointment to see a doctor, and do exactly what he or she says.

Somewhere along the line, we've lost our sense of community. Instead of leaning on each other, we've been told to seek the help of medical professionals. But the truth is that pharmaceutical companies – indeed, the entire mental health industry -- has a stake in keeping people sick. Drug companies want to sell their drugs; doctors need patients to keep coming back. And what better way to keep people coming back than to sell them the narrative that there is a pill for every ill.

Today, we have a free wheeling corporatized market system where anything goes. For profit pharmaceutical companies make drugs; the FDA approves them. Smooth-talking pharmaceutical sales representatives manipulate doctors with research to support the safety and efficacy of whatever drug they're trying to sell. Unsuspecting patients trust their doctors and do as they are told. Is it any wonder that people are being injured?

Indeed, many of the trusted pillars of our culture are, in fact, failing us. Our schools do not teach us to think critically; instead, we're taught to conform, to do as we are told, and not to ask questions. We're encouraged to choose professions that will garner the highest wages rather than to follow our dreams. We recite words to convince ourselves that we are living in a country that provides "liberty and justice for all," when in fact this is not the case. Religion teaches us that we are sinners, and we are given a rigid formula regarding the specific conditions under which -- and with whom -- we are allowed to share our bodies.

When woven together, these false narratives create a tapestry filled with too many holes. These are the stories that make people sick, and I'm no longer willing to support industries or institutions that injure people.

• • •

Many people believe I "lost my marbles" back in 2013.

And, in a way, they aren't wrong.

In general, folks would prefer to label me as "crazy" or as an "addict" rather than look at their own relationship with mood-altering substances; however, I tend to think of myself as an accidental traveler, sort of like Dorothy Gale from The Wizard of Oz.

When Dorothy starts her journey down The Yellow Brick Road, she is terrified and -- with the exception of her dog, Toto -- completely alone. A girl whose life is turned upside down after an event that is completely out of her control, she doesn't yet know that the tornado will bring unexpected gifts to her life. She doesn't know she'll make new friends and learn valuable lessons along the way; she is simply trying to survive. It is only later, when Dorothy feels safe and whole, that she is able to see how far she has come and express gratitude to those who helped her to limp along life's path.

Like Dorothy, I went through a storm – a nightmarish journey -- a transformational process to become the person I am today. My rite of passage has not been an easy one. I literally had to sacrifice my life, go to the other side, meet with Spirit guides, acquire new friends, and obtain all the information that I could gather as to why I am here on this planet. I've learned to trust the Universe to give me the information I need, without questioning or judging myself or worrying what other people think.

For five decades, people have told me to be quiet about what I see and hear, that I sound "crazy" when I talk about voices and demons, spirits and angels.

I no longer care what people think, and I refuse to be quiet when it comes to talking about what I know as lived experience. Too many individuals are currently trapped in the web of lies that is psychiatry, and when they begin to see the prison bars that surround them, I want to be there for them as others have been for me.

Over the last eight years, I've worked hard to rebuild a new life for myself after decades of complicated, repressed trauma -- made even more complicated by being pathologized by the medical community. As it turns out, there was nothing wrong with me, except for the fact that I'd spent much of my life placating others.

These days, I march to the beat of my own drum -- even if it goes against everyone else's. I'm no longer at war with the inner critic inside my head, neither am I a hostage to the past. I've stopped pushing myself to be perfect. More than anything else, this journey has been about developing patience. I'm slower than I used to be, more intentional and deliberate. I do the best I can to be of service to others without losing myself in the process.

I'm grateful for the life I have, and I choose to focus on what I have rather than what I've lost. I'm fortunate to get up every day and do what I love to do. I've had an opportunity to heal old wounds and make amends with nearly everyone who matters to me. These days, I don't push to make things happen; instead, I simply take a deep breath each morning, set an intention, do the work, and wait for the magic to come.

It always does.

The best part, though, is that I no longer feel broken or defective.

In truth, I never was.

EPILOGUE

While there is information about the dangers of long-term benzodiazepine use circulating on the Internet, it seems most doctors are not getting this information. Doctors are very good at prescribing these drugs, but they know precious little about how to safely help people to stop taking them. Because of this fact, patients need to approach doctors (and the scripts they write) with greater caution -- and doctors need to adopt a level of humility, acknowledge it is impossible to learn about each of the several thousand prescription drugs currently available, and approach their prescription pads with greater care.

Healthcare professionals must do better when it comes to listening to their patients; they must be open-minded when patients come forward with information that directly impacts their lives – even if this information comes from a seemingly obscure online group. At the most basic level, prescribing doctors need to become familiarized with The Ashton Method to help patients to more safely taper off psychiatric medications, as well as reconsider the prescription protocols they were taught back in medical school and/or residency.

I hope the next generation of medical professionals will be better informed about the nature of traumatic stress and its effect on the human brain and body so that they will be more prone to recommend non-pharmaceutical ways of dealing with panic disorders, anxiety, depression and addiction.

It also needs to be said that while my brain injury was debilitating, the "gaslighting" that I endured by the American healthcare system has also left its mark. To be clear, gaslighting -- the repeated denial of someone's reality in an attempt to invalidate or dismiss his or her experience — is a form of emotional abuse. When patients present with excruciating physical and psychological symptoms that arise as a result of coming off benzodiazepines too quickly, they are often not believed and their complaints are commonly dismissed. And when a medical professional leads a person to question his/her sanity, it can be just as traumatic and abusive as whatever brought them to the doctor in the first place. In mistakenly concluding that patients' symptoms are 'all in their head,' medical professionals delay (and possibly altogether discourage) that person from pursuing proper diagnosis and treatment.

Like others who have survived life-altering experiences, making it through benzodiazepine withdrawal has made me a kinder, more compassionate human being. I've come to understand more about myself than I ever have before.

About what makes me feel healthy and what makes me sick.

About how to tell the truth and when to tell the truth.

About how to remain a storyteller without lying.

About how and from who to accept love.

I know how to ask for help and give it, too.

There was a period where my brain was so damaged that the concept of love was just a memory of an idea. I could feel nothing at all. Many highly paid "experts" told me I was crazy, that it was "absolutely impossible" for me to still be experiencing withdrawal symptoms after six months, let alone forty-six months. And while some of the best conventional minds told me I was mad, there were others who knew better.

People reached out to me and told me that I would be okay.

They taught me about neuroplasticity and encouraged me to hold on for another moment. They reassured me that, eventually, all the tiny moments would add up into minutes, then hours, then days.

They told me there would be days where I would go backwards, where my symptoms would intensify. They told me healing is not linear.

I've always believed in angels, and I believe — more than ever – that we are all surrounded by a powerful, invisible magic: a blend of science and faith, which shows us that anything is possible.

Is my life perfect now?

Of course not. I still have struggles and insecurities. But my problems are no longer paralyzing to me, and when bad things happen, I have people upon whom I can rely and tools I can use to stay grounded.

We live in a culture that demands we hide our pain. Whether it is physical or emotional, we are encouraged to move through difficult life circumstances quickly and, often, we are shamed when we try to slow down to take care of ourselves.

Unfortunately, processing trauma cannot be rushed. If someone is grieving the end of a relationship - a death or divorce – or going through a period of intense stress, it takes time to transition through these emotions.

Over the last eight years, I've met many healers. They are out there, walking around on the planet, individuals with the knowledge and the tools to help us to "ungunk our spiritual pipes," to teach us how to ground ourselves during turbulent times, to reconnect with our intuition, to return to heart-center, and to help us to heal our deepest wounds.

If only I had known sooner.

GLOSSARY

AKATHESIA

A movement disorder characterized by a subjective feeling of inner restlessness accompanied by mental distress and an inability to sit still. Usually, the legs are most prominently affected. Those affected may fidget, rock back and forth, or pace, while some may just have an uneasy feeling in their body.

ASHTON METHOD

Best known for her clinical and research work on benzodiazepine dependence, Crystal Heather Ashton was a British psychopharmacologist and physician. Ashton's findings led to her write a manual to help those who were trying to stop their prescribed benzodiazepine. First published in 1999, her book - *Benzodiazepines: How They Work and How to Withdraw* - is known as *The Ashton Manual* and has been translated into eleven languages.

ATAXIA

The loss of full control of bodily movement.

"COLD TURKEY"

Slang term used to describe the abrupt cessation of a drug that can lead to severe withdrawal severe withdrawal symptoms, seizures, even death.

DYSTONIA

A state of abnormal muscle tone resulting in muscular spasm and abnormal posture, typically due to neurological disease or a side effect of drug therapy.

EYE MOVEMENT DESENSITIZATION & REPROCESSING (EMDR)

A structured therapy that encourages patients to briefly focus on a traumatic memory while simultaneously experiencing bilateral stimulation (typically eye movements), which -- when administered properly, are associated with a reduction in the vividness and emotion associated with traumatic memories.

EMOTIONAL FREEDOM TECHNIQUE (EFT) TAPPING

An alternative treatment for physical pain and emotional distress, EFT tapping is used to restore balance to a person's disrupted energy. An authorized treatment for war veterans with PTSD, it's demonstrated some benefits as a treatment for anxiety, depression, physical pain, and insomnia.

INTERDOSE WITHDRAWAL

When people who are prescribed benzodiazepines become physically dependent by taking them beyond the 2-4 week recommended time frame, they sometimes experience withdrawal symptoms that emerge in between scheduled doses.

KINDLING

The process of being put on and taken off numerous psychotropic drugs triggers a neurological condition, which occurs as a result of repeated exposure and cessation episodes from any drug that affects the central nervous system. Each withdrawal leads to more severe symptoms than in previous episodes, and kindled individuals are at an increased risk of severe withdrawal symptoms, up to and including seizures and death. Benzodiazepines are especially notorious for causing kindling.

MYOFASCIAL RELEASE (MR)

A type of physical therapy often used to treat chronic pain caused by sensitivity and tightness in your myofascial tissues. These tissues surround and support the muscles throughout your body. The pain usually originates from specific points within your myofascial tissues called "trigger points."

NEUROLEPTIC DRUGS

A class of psychotropic medication primarily used to manage a range of psychotic disorders. Recent research has shown that use of any antipsychotic drugs results in smaller brain tissue volumes and that this brain shrinkage is dose and time dependent.

PARADOXICAL REACTION

An outcome that is opposite from the outcome that would be expected from a drug's known actions.

PROTRACTED or POST ACUTE WITHDRAWAL SYNDROME (PAWS)

PAWS occurs in patients who have withdrawn from benzodiazepines and continue to experience long-term withdrawal effects. The term 'protracted' refers to the time duration, describing withdrawal symptoms which persist for months and even years after benzodiazepine cessation. These protracted symptoms occur due to functional changes within the neuro-receptors and areas of the central nervous system that benzodiazepines affect.

REIKI

A healing technique based on the principle that the therapist can channel energy into the patient by means of touch, to activate the natural healing processes of the patient's body and restore physical and emotional well being.

SOMATO RESPIRO INTEGRATION (SRI)

Created by Dr. Donald Epstein, SRI is a series of exercises using breath, awareness, touch and movement developed to help an individual connect one's body and mind. When administered properly, SRI helps an individual to connect with his/her innate wisdom which can help that individual to better handle life's challenges more effectively.

TARDIVE DYSKINESIA

A neurological disorder characterized by involuntary movements of the face and jaw.

TOLERANCE

Tolerance occurs when a person no longer responds to a drug in the way they did at first. So it takes a higher dose of the drug to achieve the same effect as when the person first used it. This is why people with substance use disorders use more and more of a drug to get the desired effect they seek.

RESOURCES

Benzo Free Podcast with D.E. Foster.

Benzodiazepine Awareness Podcast with Geraldine Burns.

Breggin, Peter & David Cohen. *Your Drug May Be Your Problem, Revised Edition: How & Why to Stop Taking Psychiatric Medications*. Da Capo Lifelong Books; Revised edition. July 2007.

Carter, Rosalynn. Within Our Reach: Ending the Mental Health Crisis. Rodale Books; 1st edition. April 2010.

Cunningham, Lynn & Wendy Ractliffe. *Medicating Normal. Periscope Films. 2020.*

Foster, D.E. Benzo Free: The World of Anti-Anxiety Drugs & The Reality of Withdrawal. Denim Mountain Press. Aug 2018.

Frederick, Baylissa. *Recovery and Renewal:* Your Essential Guide to Overcoming Dependency & Withdrawal from Sleeping Pills, Other 'Benzo' Tranquillizers & Antidepressants. RRW Publishing; Updated edition, April 2017.

Halligan, Patricia. Recovery: *The Hero's Journey Podcast.* Voice America.

Lembke, Anna. *Drug Dealer, MD: How Doctors Were Duped, Patients Got Hooked, & Why It's So Hard to Stop.* Johns Hopkins University Press. Nov 2016.

Ling, Lisa. "This is Life. "The Benzo Crisis." *YouTube. Season 6, Episode 2. Oct 2019.*

Peterson, Mikhaila. *The Mikhaila Peterson Podcast.* "The Dangers of Psychiatric Medication, featuring Dr. Jim Wright & Dr. David Cohen.*" YouTube. Episode 83. May 2021.*

ORGANIZATIONS

The Akathisia Alliance for Education & Research
The Alliance for Benzodiazepine Best Practices
Benzodiazepine Action Work Group
Benzodiazepine Information Coalition
Benzo Free
Benzo.org.uk
The Withdrawal Project by Inner Compass Initiative
World Benzodiazepine Awareness Day

ACKNOWLEDGMENTS

My mother always said me she'd hoped I'd write a book some day. I'm not sure this is the kind of book she was dreaming of, but here it is. Deepest and most profound thanks to my parents, **Philip** and **Joan Schuls**, for standing beside me always and forever -- even when I am talking about the hard stuff.

To **Bobbi Wilkins** for allowing me to read to her, draft after draft aloud, over the telephone. Her endless encouragement and willingness to wordsmith helped me to get through each and every draft.

To **Regina Barnello Wright, Renee Beck McLain and the rest of the McLain crew -- Madison, Emily, Audrey and Harry; Patricia Halligan, Vickijo Campanero, Maria de la Cruz, & Bruce Gilberg**: I'm truly grateful to each of you for allowing me to use your real names and likenesses in my memoir. Thank you for being there for me when I was at my lowest low.

To my ex-husband and our son, **Calvin**: I know this memoir is painful to read in parts, and I truly appreciate your willingness to allow me to share this story with the world. You will always be my family.

To my beta readers: **Emily Schuls, Linda Mazur, Nina Badzin, Lisha Fink, Katie Kiss, Susan Bielat** & **Christy Huff**, each of whom offered valued perspectives during the editing process.

To **Monica Cassani**, one of the first people I found when I began researching the topic of benzodiazepine withdrawal. Her blog "Everything Matters: Beyond Meds" was truly the first step on my healing journey. Soon after, **Don Killian** offered me emotional support on a near-daily basis when I was in post-acute benzodiazepine withdrawal. "How do you know that I'm going to be okay?" I'd weep. "What if I'm worse than everyone else?" He always responded in a calm, reassuraning tone. "Because I thought I was the worst case scenario, and I have healed – and you will, too." Thank goodness he was right.

I'd like to acknowledge **Paul Chomiak**, a fellow survivor and Chief Hellfire Layman Pirate when it comes to benzodiazepines. He manages several online support groups and keeps track of any and all published articles that pertain to psychotropic drugs and the harm they cause. To all the volunteers at the Benzodiazepine Information Coaltion. How I wish that organization had been around in 2004 before I filled that script.

And finally, thanks to my counselors at The Meadows of Wickenberg and to all the people I met there who reflected back to me something that I could not yet see for myself.

ENDNOTES

---

[1] "A Brief History of Benzodiazepines." *Benzodiazepine Information Coalition*. https://www.benzoinfo.com/a-brief-history-of-benzodiazepines/.

[2] Wick JY. The history of benzodiazepines. Consult Pharm. 2013 Sep; 28(9):538-48. doi: 10.4140/TCP.n.2013.538. PMID: 24007886. https://pubmed.ncbi.nlm.nih.gov/24007886/.

[3] Brown, M. Lewis, S. (2021). The Patient Voice: Antidepressant Withdrawal, Medically Unexplained Symptoms, and Functional Neurological Disorders. *Journal of Critical Psychology, Counselling, and Psychotherapy, 20* (4), 14-20.

[4] Pies, Ronald W. "Debunking the Two Chemical Imbalance Myths, Again." *Psychiatric Times*, Vol 36, Issue 8, Volume 36, Issue 8. 2 Aug 2019. https://www.psychiatrictimes.com/view/debunking-two-chemical-imbalance-myths-again

[5] Kenny, Shane. "New FDA Study Shows Benzodiazepines Can Cause Long-Term Injury." Mad In America. Published Online: 2 Dec 2020. https://www.madinamerica.com/2020/12/fda-benzo-cause-injury.

[6] Pétursson H. "The benzodiazepine withdrawal syndrome." 1994 Nov; 89(11):1455-9. doi: 10.1111/j.1360-0443.1994.tb03743.x. PMID: 7841856. https://pubmed.ncbi.nlm.nih.gov/7841856/.

[7] Ostrow, Laysha et al. "Discontinuing Psychiatric Medications: A Survey of Long-Term Users." *Psychiatric Services*. Published Online:17 Jul 2017. https://doi.org/10.1176/appi.ps.201700070 pp. 1232-1238.

[8] Cheng, Hui M et al. "Akathisia: a life-threatening side effect of a common medication." *BMJ case reports* vol. 2013 bcr2012007713. 21 May. 2013, doi: 10.1136/bcr-2012-007713. https://www.ncbi.nlm.nih.gov/pmc/articles/PMC3670081/.

[9] Whitaker, Robert. *Anatomy of an Epidemic*: Magic Bullets, Psychiatric Drugs, and the Astonishing Rise of Mental Illness in America. New York: Crown Publishers, 2010.

ABOUT THE AUTHOR

Renée A. Schuls-Jacobson graduated from Hobart & William Smith Colleges (1989) and University of Buffalo (1992). Eight years after her iatrogenic injury, Renée's brain has mostly healed. Today, she is an independent artist whose paintings hang in private collections throughout the world. In addition to making and selling her artwork, it has become her mission to educate the public about the dangers associated with long-term psychiatric drug use. A Certified Recovery Peer Advocate, she offers emotional support to people who are suffering through protracted benzodiazepine and SSRI withdrawal syndrome. Her home and studio are located in Rochester, New York.

Made in the USA
Columbia, SC
01 August 2021